When Play Isn't Fun

Helping Children Resolve Play Conflicts

SANDRA HEIDEMANN and DEBORAH HEWITT

Name:_____

Date:_____

Redleaf Press®
www.redleafpress.org
800-423-8309

Also from Redleaf Press by Sandra Heidemann and Deborah Hewitt:
When Play Isn't Easy: Helping Children Enter and Sustain Play
Play: The Pathway from Theory to Practice, revised edition of *Pathways to Play*

From Deborah Hewitt:

So This Is Normal Too?, second edition

Published by Redleaf Press
10 Yorkton Court
St. Paul, MN 55117
www.redleafpress.org

© 2014 by Sandra Heidemann and Deborah Hewitt

First edition 2014
Cover design by Erin New
Cover photographs by © iStock/Ljupco Smokovski
Interior design by Erin New
Typeset in Adobe Garamond Pro and Futura
Printed in the United States of America
21 20 19 18 17 16 15 14   1 2 3 4 5 6 7 8

Library of Congress Cataloging-in-Publication Data
Heidemann, Sandra, 1946-
  When play isn't fun : helping children resolve play conflicts / Sandra Heidemann, Deborah Hewitt.
       pages cm
    Summary: "This book will broaden your knowledge about the important topic of play, and it will help you explore common challenges children might experience in play. Hands-on techniques, assessments, reflection questions, and exercises are included to help you more effectively support and strengthen children's play"
  — Provided by publisher.
    ISBN 978-1-60554-305-5 (paperback)
    1. Play—Psychological aspects. 2. Education, Preschool. 3. Child psychology.
4. Child development.   I. Hewitt, Debbie, 1958- II. Title.
  LB1139.35.P55H45 2014
  303.3'2—dc23
                                        2013044405

Printed on acid-free paper

Contents

Dear Reader,

This book and its companion reflect a renewed interest in play and how very important it is in the healthy development of children. In this new world of technology, play continues to be the most powerful force for learning in a young child's life. And our job as people who teach young children is to provide the best environment for play to happen. This book, *When Play Isn't Fun: Helping Children Resolve Play Conflicts,* focuses on setting up your environment, schedule, and curriculum for play and highlights several group-play challenges and how to address them. The companion book, *When Play Isn't Easy: Helping Children Enter and Sustain Play,* offers a detailed look at the Play Checklist introduced in our book *Play: The Pathway from Theory to Practice,* plus an exploration of how play connects to early learning standards. The books build on information from *Play* and can be an additional resource to it. The books move from designing your learning environment to maximize play, to helping groups of children resolve barriers to more productive play, to helping individual children learn better play skills. The books could be used on your own, with your teaching team, or by your organization. They could be the basis of workshops.

As we began these books, we decided to ask friends and family about their experiences with play. Their memories are touching, funny, and poignant. Many of their quotes are included in the books.

Those of us who care for children have many possible roles: teacher, assistant teacher, aide, family child care provider, specialist, and others. We all interact with children as they play. We have chosen to use the term *teacher* when referring to all adults working in our field. We are all teachers in each of our roles. The suggestions are valuable whatever your title.

We have used the term *learning environment* to refer to the variety of settings we see in early childhood.

We hope these books help you to remember your own play experiences and use those memories to strengthen the play experiences for the children in your care. As you increase your intentionality with regard to play in your learning environment, children will show you their delight in new and fascinating ways.

Sandy & Debbie

Introduction

Whether you are a teacher, teacher assistant, or a family child care provider, you have seen children playing with enthusiasm. Children find ways to play together in classrooms, dramatic play areas, outdoor playgrounds, and on living room floors. You have also seen children's play end in tears or fights over toys. Despite these conflicts and angry moments, children want to play together and you have an important role in making it happen. Perhaps you are not always clear about your role. You may have many questions about what play is, what children are learning, and how you can help children reach a more mature level of play. This book answers these questions, outlines strategies to create an engaging play environment, helps you understand play skill development, and suggests ways you can encourage children's growth through play. It also covers challenges children have during play, such as conflicts over toys and violent play, and how you address them. You could complete this book as an individual to improve your strategies around play, as a teaching team seeking better ways to work together on play environments, as an entire center organizing around a goal of strengthening play in your classrooms, or as a learning community or class studying children's play. However you approach the book, you will find ideas to make play come alive and give children a powerful way to learn and grow.

☀ Nadia, a teacher in the four-year-old room, sat at a table and smiled at the busy activity around her. It was free-choice time and children were playing in several interest centers. A group of four children was in the house area setting the table and fixing dinner, another group was in the block area constructing an airport, and several children were signing cards in the writing center. The cards were going in the class mailbox when the children were finished.

Setting the Stage for Play

Maybe if you were Nadia you would feel grateful that the children were involved and busy. However, experiences like this do not just happen. Nadia took an active role in making this successful play happen in her room because she believes young children grow and thrive through play.

Time to Reflect

You too have an important role in setting the stage for play in your learning environment. What do you think Nadia did to set the stage for play?

_____

_____

_____

_____

You might have noted the activities she set up or the interest areas she designed, but there are other ways Nadia helped children engage in play. She paid attention to how much time she allotted to free-choice time, she carefully chose props and materials that encouraged a range of involvement, and she helped children collect new props or solve conflicts with each other. Before she even began planning space and choosing toys, she had learned how play skills develop and how to observe children as they play.

Children Need Adult Support

If you set the stage for play with goals in mind, you will ensure children gain the kind of play experiences they need to develop and thrive. Children learn more if adults support their play in the following ways:

- Understand how play skills develop.
- Observe children as they play.
- Set up the play space.
- Include engaging and varying props.
- Provide enough time for play.
- Facilitate friendships.
- Help solve conflicts.

SELF-ASSESSMENT

Are you doing everything you can to help set the stage for play? Self-assessments help us look at ourselves and how our own attitudes and beliefs can affect our practices. Take the following self-assessment to learn more about how you put your beliefs and knowledge about play into action:

1 I am aware of how memories of my own childhood play experiences influence my work with children (chapter 1).

    a) Always   b) Usually   c) Sometimes   d) Never

2 I observe children while they play and write down my observations so I can identify what stage they are in (chapter 2).

    a) Always   b) Usually   c) Sometimes   d) Never

3 I arrange my learning environment into interest areas, including one for dramatic play (chapter 3).

    a) Always   b) Usually   c) Sometimes   d) Never

4 I provide enough time for play (chapter 3).

    a) Always   b) Usually   c) Sometimes   d) Never

5 I may get discouraged when encountering a problem, but I stick with it until I find a solution (chapter 4).

    a) Always   b) Usually   c) Sometimes   d) Never

6 When I try one strategy to help children play together and it doesn't work, I plan to use another one (chapter 4).

    a) Always   b) Usually   c) Sometimes   d) Never

7 I use problem-solving steps with children when they are fighting with each other (chapter 5).

    a) Always   b) Usually   c) Sometimes   d) Never

8 When children aren't using the dramatic play area, I join in the play to get them started (chapter 6).

    a) Always   b) Usually   c) Sometimes   d) Never

9 When children make up violent stories, I make sure it is safe for all, and talk with the children about their feelings (chapter 7).

    a) Always   b) Usually   c) Sometimes   d) Never

10 I help children pretend to be superheroes if the play is safe and creative (chapter 7).

    a) Always   b) Usually   c) Sometimes   d) Never

Your self-assessment is a snapshot of what you know about play and how you help children experiencing challenges during play. Your responses can point to areas you want to strengthen.

Time to Reflect

When you look over your self-assessment, do you have questions or thoughts? What would you like to learn more about?

_____

_____

_____

_____

Using This Book

The book is divided into eight chapters. Chapter 1 asks you to consider your own childhood play experiences and how they influence your reactions to children's play. Chapters 2 and 3 review how children's play skills develop and, given that, how you can design and facilitate exciting and engaging dramatic play areas. Chapter 4 delves into how you approach problems and outlines a problem-solving approach that you can apply to your work. Chapters 5 through chapter 8 examine various group play challenges, such as violent or repetitive play, that keep children from experiencing the richness of group play. Each chapter contains suggestions as well as reflection questions to help you find workable strategies.

This book is designed to be interactive and is meant to encourage thought, reflection, and discussion. As you reflect on and then plan and implement new play strategies, you become a more intentional teacher providing children with rich play experiences.

Remembering Your Play Experiences CHAPTER 1

Remembering your childhood play experiences will help you empathize with children as they seek out new friends, latch on to special play themes and toys, and experience hurt feelings over being excluded. Your play history is part of what you bring to your interactions with children.

When you recall your play experiences, you may remember playing in your neighborhood or home with little or no adult supervision. Perhaps your outdoor play included natural materials such as mud to represent cooking, leaves to represent fish, and porch railings to represent horses. With your friends, you could have acted out elaborate themes of war or adventure and not wanted to stop when called in for supper. You and your friends might have taken risks by climbing, running, hiding, and crawling on the ground, resulting in physical injuries. You may remember hurtful words, fights, and being left out as you worked out your conflicts with other children.

The unstructured play just described has great benefits for children and often occupies a special place as adults recall play memories. However, you cannot duplicate this type of play in your learning environment. Safety regulations and your active presence in the learning environment mean the play experiences of the children in your setting will be different. The children may still have play experiences in their homes and neighborhoods similar to the ones you remember from your childhood, but because you provide structure and supervision, they will have more support to work out conflicts, more planned play experiences, and more adult input in your setting. You can still provide some of the benefits of less structured play while keeping children safe both emotionally and physically. The following chart highlights how you can bring the benefits of less structured play into your learning environment.

BRINGING IN LESS STRUCTURED PLAY

What Adults Remember	What You Can Provide
Having Choices Adults remember being able to choose play activities.	Give children choices of activities and toys. Save enough time in your schedule to play and explore those activities. Listen to their interests and provide a dramatic play theme based on those interests.
Playing Outdoors Adults remember playing outdoors with natural materials.	Bring your dramatic play outside. You could even set several interest areas outside. Take walks and explore the natural environment. Set up a children's garden plot in the summer months.
Confronting Challenges Adults remember overcoming physical and emotional challenges.	Encourage children to try activities that are out of their comfort zone. Provide support to continue trying until they succeed.
Solving Their Own Conflicts Adults remember solving conflicts with their playmates, often without any adult support.	Although you want children to feel emotionally safe and to seek your assistance when they have conflict, encourage them to find solutions and try them out.
Learning through Mistakes Adults remember making many mistakes while playing, but learning through them.	Don't be too quick to jump in and rescue a child who is making mistakes. Offer assistance when the child is too frustrated, but applaud all attempts to overcome challenges.

Fond Play Memories

You probably have many fond memories of the toys you played with, the places you chose to play, and the special friend or groups of friends who joined you. However, adults often remember little from their preschool years and tend to think of how they played as older children. Try to think of your earliest experiences with play. You may recall a toy you loved or a play space that you revisited over and over again.

Time to Reflect

Think of a fun play experience you had when you were a young child, then answer the following questions:

Where were you playing?

_____

_____

What were you playing?

_____

_____

What toys were you playing with?

_____

_____

Were you alone or with other children?

_____

_____

What made it especially fun for you?

_____

_____

I remember playing with a group of stuffed animals. I often played alone because I was the oldest child and didn't have siblings until I was five years old. These stuffed animals became my friends, and I made up story after story about their adventures. They talked to each other and probably fought. I often gathered them around me and showed them my Golden Books. I smile even now as I think of a particular bear, my favorite. —Sandy

I particularly liked playing pretend. I liked to play store and school and college. (Yeah, that one was kind of weird. I wonder where we even got the idea for that one.) I think my favorite part was setting up the staging area. I liked to have my own space, such as a store or classroom or dorm room. And I liked to very carefully arrange all my pretend possessions in the space. In the winter, my friends and I would even play house in the snow. We would build walls with little nooks to hold certain items like pinecones. —Marcia

In the wide gully next to our house on the edge of town sat a big tree that had been split by lightning, with one long, thick section of the trunk lying horizontally and suspended by branches a couple of feet off the ground. The tree became a fort from which we repelled outlaws or other enemies depending on the historical period we imagined. —Steve M.

Difficult Play Memories

Play can be fun, but it also can be painful or discouraging. Children fight over toys, friends, and rules. Children can feel left out and may not fit into the group. Children may get hurt, either emotionally or physically.

Time to Reflect

Think about a time you were sad or upset as a young child while playing. Answer the questions below:

Where were you playing?

_____

_____

_____

_____

What were you playing?

_____

_____

_____

_____

What toys were you playing with?

_____

_____

_____

_____

Were you alone or with other children?

_____

_____

What made it especially painful for you?

_____

_____

_____

_____

What would you have liked to have happen differently?

_____

_____

_____

_____

I was not very athletic growing up, or maybe I just wasn't aggressive enough to play team sports. I used to love kickball and tetherball, but team sports always made me a bit nervous. I never wanted to fail or be embarrassed if I wasn't good enough. —Sarah

We moved every year, sometimes twice a year, until I was thirteen. It wasn't fun to be the new kid. —Steve S.

I remember getting pulled around by my hair while fighting over toys, and I hated feeling left out when playing with a group of kids. —Carrie

During recess in elementary school, my classmates were playing a game of kickball and choosing teams. I was the last one to be picked, and neither one wanted me on their team. I remember running from the playground in tears to talk to the playground monitor/teacher. —Lisa

Why Do Your Childhood Experiences Matter?

Although you may not always be aware of it, your past play experiences influence how you interpret children's play.

☀ Marion, a teacher in a four-year-old room, observed three girls having an argument in the house area. Two of the girls were telling the third one she couldn't play there and they didn't want to play with her. Marion found herself becoming angry and resentful of the two girls excluding the other girl. She went to a coworker to complain. As they talked, Marion remembered a time she had been excluded from a special friendship with two other girls. She felt hurt and angry as she remembered that experience. When she realized the connection between her past experiences and the girls' situation, she was able to put her own feelings aside and focus on how to help the girls find a solution.

Clearly some of Marion's anger from her past experience was coloring how she saw the girls' conflict. Without understanding her own reaction, she may have handled this conflict in a harsher or more punishing manner, instead of helping the girls resolve their dilemma. Painful play experiences can influence your interactions years later. Understanding your own strong reactions can help you focus your interactions on what children need to learn to play successfully.

> Memories of your play experiences can range from the very pleasant to the very sad or something in between. As you set up the play environment or interact with children in play, you bring your memories into your teaching, whether you remember them consciously or not.

Time to Reflect

How do you think your childhood play experiences influence how you plan and implement play opportunities for the children you teach?

_____

_____

_____

_____

If Marion had come to you with her observations about the three girls, how would you have responded to her feelings?

_____

_____

_____

_____

Understanding the Pathways to Play

Children go through developmental stages as they learn to play. These stages are marked by two pathways: (1) how children relate to objects or toys and (2) how children relate to peers or friends. As babies, children are already beginning to explore objects and form relationships with adults through play. Their play increasingly becomes more and more sophisticated until they are eventually able to combine both pathways into imaginative dramatic play experiences during the preschool years. Although growth in the two pathways is happening simultaneously, it's helpful to examine them separately to better understand each pathway and how to support it.

Time to Reflect

Think about special toys or materials you had in childhood. What did you do with them? What made them special?

_____

_____

_____

_____

> Content in this chapter connects with chapter 2 in *Play: The Pathway from Theory to Practice.*

Play with Objects

You may become very nostalgic when you remember special toys from your childhood. Perhaps you loved your toy because someone you loved gave it you. Or maybe you saw an advertisement for a toy and knew you wanted it. Perhaps the toy reminded you of your home and your parents. Toys are very important to children. A special toy almost becomes a part of a child's identity. Although adults are not always aware of why a particular toy is important to a child, it is important to respect it and explore it with the child. Objects serve important functions for children, and they use them in several ways:

They explore. When babies first begin to hold objects in their hands, they explore how an object feels, how it moves, and how it sounds. Even after infancy, the first thing children do with a new toy is explore it. They first want to know what it does, how it moves, and how it feels. Then they may be ready to pretend with it.

They construct. As children move into the preschool years they want to build with blocks, Tinkertoys, and bristle blocks. They stack them, build towers, and put them together to make pretend machines. As toddlers, children stack just a few blocks; as they get older, they put together large buildings and long roads to drive on.

They pretend. Children begin pretending between twelve months and eighteen months by performing one action. They may pick up a toy phone and pretend to listen or pat a doll, pretending it is a baby. As they get older they string together several actions to form an actual story, their story. So they may pick up the baby, pat it, feed it, and put it in the crib to sleep. When they are very young, they need real or real-looking objects to play out their action, but as they get older they can substitute or even use imaginary actions to pretend. You may have seen children give baby dolls pretend food or pretend to eat with their fingers.

PLAY WITH OBJECTS

Stage	Definition	Examples
Sensorimotor	Exploring object by mouthing, pounding, shaking, and turning	Child shakes rattle Child puts objects in mouth Child rolls ball
Constructive	Building with blocks or manipulatives such as Lego blocks	Child builds a simple tower Child builds a road Child makes an enclosure or fence Child makes a city
Dramatic Play	Using objects to pretend or act out roles	Child pretends to make a phone call with a toy phone Child gives adult imaginary money Child pretends to be a teacher

I loved Groovy Girls! I played with them like they were dolls and made pretend houses for them under chairs. Once I cut one's hair. I pretended like they were talking to each other. —Katie, age 10

I had a number of toys that I pretty much loved to death. There was a teddy bear and a bunny and a rag doll that an aunt made for me. I spent a lot of time pretending I was a teacher and my toys were the class. I really enjoyed explaining things to them. —JoAnn

In the fall months we would play with marbles (*cincos*), tops (*trompos*), and kites—you can only fly kites in November because if you start to fly a kite in August, then they would say that you were scaring the rain away, so you had to wait. Depending on your family's economic condition, some bought kites and some made them. In my case, I made them with newspaper (the classifieds, because it was yellow, and other ads that had colors). I made them out of alternative materials, whatever was available. —Edgar, from Guatemala

☀ Chelsea was a two-year-old girl who had just started in Mimi's family child care home. She seemed to be adjusting well but insisted on bringing a stuffed bunny from home with her every day. She carried it around all day and cried whenever she had to put it down to eat or wash her hands. Mimi was concerned Chelsea wasn't playing with the other children because she was so worried about the bunny and where it was. Mimi knew children had toys they bring from home to child care to help them make the transition between the two places. But this didn't seem to be working for Chelsea. After a couple of weeks Mimi decided to make a special place for the bunny on a shelf. She asked Chelsea to put the bunny on the shelf where she could see it anytime she wanted. She could also hold it, but afterward the bunny would sit in its special spot. The first day Chelsea asked to see and hold it several times during the day, but gradually, she would look at the bunny and then run to play with her new friends.

Time to Reflect

What kinds of toys or objects have you seen children grow attached to?

_____

_____

_____

_____

How do you handle children like Chelsea who need transition objects between home and your setting?

_____

_____

_____

_____

If you haven't allowed a child a transition object before, how might you do so in the future?

_____

_____

_____

_____

Encouraging Play with a Variety of Objects

There continues to be great controversy over the fact that some toys are marketed to girls and others are marketed to boys. When you walk in store aisles, you probably see "girls" rows and "boys" rows. The girls' rows have pink and purple items. They are filled with dolls, doll clothes, and tea sets. The boys' rows have action figures, Lego blocks, and more active toys in darker blues, grays, and black. Even baby toys are color-coded. Pink is for girls and blue is for boys. It may be easy to inadvertently allow these gender stereotypes to occur in your learning environment. You may see girls gravitate to the house area and the boys preferring the block area. It's unknown exactly how boys and girls learn these preferences. Is it something they learn through media, advertising, and social expectations, or are there genetic differences in object preferences?

Regardless, in early childhood settings it is important to offer all children opportunities for play with all types of toys. Offer toys that attract both boys and girls. If boys are always in the block area, put out family figures, a dollhouse, or toy animals to bring more girls in. If girls are dominating the house area, make sure there are roles available for boys and encourage them to go shopping for groceries and to hold the baby. Reducing gender stereotypes in play gives all children a chance to explore a variety of experiences and challenges.

☀ One morning I was observing in a classroom of four-year-old children. I watched a girl take every single container of manipulatives and dump them on top of the shelf. The shelf was full of small multicolored objects. As the teacher approached the child, I wondered how she would handle this overwhelming "mess." I thought she might ask the child to clean it up and stop the dumping. Instead she bent down to the child's level and asked her what she was doing. The child smiled and exclaimed excitedly, "I'm doing a jewelry store." The teacher asked other children to come over and play jewelry store. Several children came over to buy jewelry, and others helped the girl sell it. They paused over the small objects and talked about how pretty they were.

Sometimes you may not be sure what a child is pretending. By stopping and asking the girl what she was pretending with the manipulatives, the teacher facilitated a delightful experience for the children.

Time to Reflect

What did you like to play with others, and what did you like to play alone when you were a child?

_____

_____

_____

_____

Play with Others

You have seen how preschool children are drawn to playing with their peers. Even as babies, however, they have already learned many things about relationships through their interactions with adults. By relating to the adults in their lives, they learn about conversation, reading feelings, and playing games.

Children grow in their abilities to form relationships with their peers. You may have seen a child run to play with a special friend, fight with a classmate over a toy, or bond with another over a fun activity. Developing friendships is one of children's most challenging and rewarding tasks in early childhood and can be facilitated in a number of ways.

Young children go through predictable stages as they learn to play with others, from infants as they play with adults to preschoolers learning to play with friends in a group:

Playing with adults. Babies learn about play with others from the adults who care for them. They learn how to smile, how to coo back and forth, and how to play games such as so big and patty-cake. Without that foundation, children find it more difficult to enter into friendships as they get older.

Playing alone: solitary play. As children enter toddlerhood, they often play alone. They may sit and build with blocks or cook in the house area. Solitary play doesn't disappear when a child gets older. Preschoolers may also play alone at times. They may choose to sit at a computer alone or look at a book alone. Playing alone can give a child a break from a stimulating environment.

Playing beside peers: parallel play. As toddlers and young three-year-olds, children stand or sit side by side and play next to each other, but not with each other. Sometimes you are not even sure if they notice one another. There is little apparent interaction.

Playing by borrowing ideas: associative play. Slowly children move beyond parallel play and notice those around them. Although they still aren't interacting much with their peers, they are noticing what others are doing with the toys. For example, one child may be building a road in the block area. Another child may notice that road and decide to build her own road, but they remain separate roads.

Playing together: cooperative play. Around the age of three, children begin to play together in a group. The children decide to connect the roads to make a big highway to drive on. They may build cities or airports together. Sometimes children engaging in cooperative play will pretend to be a family in the house area. One child may be cooking and setting the table and others may hold babies. Cooperative play may or may not involve pretend play. Sometimes children are building or playing games together and sometimes they are pretending, but it is always with a group of children who plan their play together.

PLAY WITH OTHERS

Stages	Definitions	Examples
Play with Adults	Interacting with parents and caregivers in playful manner	Child plays so big or patty-cake Child coos back and forth with adult
Solitary Play	Playing alone with toys	Child builds a building in block corner alone Child writes at writing center alone
Parallel Play	Engaging in independent play near or next to other children	Child plays at water table next to other children Child rolls playdough at table next to other children
Associative Play	Borrowing ideas from other children while playing near them	Child builds road after watching another child build a road Child pours water out after watching other children pour from the pitcher at the water table
Cooperative Play	Playing in groups of four to five children in a cooperative fashion	Children build an airport together Children play fire station together Children play a math game together

Time to Reflect

Describe two situations where children were playing together, one where they were playing well together and one where they were having difficulty.

_____

_____

_____

_____

How Play Supports Children's Overall Development

Children use their quickly developing skills in all the developmental areas as they play. Children use language to help describe their imaginary objects. They use fine-motor skills when they pretend to write an order in the restaurant. They use emotional regulation to sustain play with their friends. They use problem-solving skills when they encounter a challenging situation, either with a friend or in finding the right prop for their play scene. All the different ways a child is developing during this period of rapid growth are expressed during play. Children's play with objects and play with others develop together. For example, when a baby plays with a parent, the focus is often on a toy. Children play in groups interacting with props and toys during cooperative play.

I loved my stuffed animals, Smurfs, and Cabbage Patch Kids. My friends and I would set up houses—well, really entire neighborhoods—and develop elaborate soap opera–like stories we acted out with our toys. I remember acting out story lines from books like the Sweet Valley High series (which my friend, who was a year older and hence much more mature than I, told me about) and made-for-TV movies. —Carrie

One of my favorite memories of play is when we lived in New Jersey and our yard bordered on the woods. My best friend, Nancy, and I would take our little dolls and small animals, furniture, whatever props we used with our dolls, and create homes, dishes, beds, and clothing for all of our "characters" with the leaves and sticks and acorn caps we found around us and then act out various dramas among the dolls and animals. We would spend hours and hours doing this. —Beth

☼ Several three- and four-year-old children were playing in the block area. Two boys were building ramps and rolling cars down them. Although they played separately, they watched each other. Often when one tried a new idea, such as leaning the ramp against a chair, the other child would do it too. Three children were pulling blocks off the shelf and onto a square on the floor. They placed the pretend steering wheel in the middle. One child exclaimed, "I'll be the driver. To get on you have to have tickets." Another child ran to the writing center, located some paper, and handed pieces to the other children. They stood in a line until the driver said they could get on the bus. One child sat by himself building a tower.

What Stages of Play Do You See?

There are three separate play scenarios happening in the preceding block-area example:
1. Using ramps
2. Riding a bus
3. Building a tower

Answer the following questions about the stages of play the children were engaged in. Although some of them may have more than one answer, choose the one that best describes the stage.

Play with Objects

1. The children riding the bus were engaged in _____.

   a) dramatic play   b) sensorimotor play   c) constructive play

2. The children playing with the ramps were engaged in _____.

   a) dramatic play   b) constructive play   c) sensorimotor play

Play with Others

3. The children playing with ramps were engaged in _____.

   a) cooperative play   b) parallel play   c) associative play

4. The child building the tower was engaged in _____.

   a) cooperative play   b) solitary play   c) parallel play

Answers: 1 = a, 2 = b, 3 = c, and 4 = b

Were these your answers? If they differed, how did they differ?

_____

_____

_____

_____

A Special Kind of Cooperative Play: Sociodramatic Play

As children deepen in their imaginary play with objects and play with others, around the age of three or four they put it all together. They play together in a group focused on a dramatic play theme. They use roles, pretend with objects, and act out a story line. You may see this in the house area as two children become the parents, one becomes the baby, and one becomes the dog. Maybe your dramatic play area is a fire station and several children pretend to put out a fire, while one runs in to save the baby. This play is called sociodramatic play. It is defined by the following elements:

Pretend play with objects. Children use objects to pretend while acting out the story. A child will put pretend money in your hand while buying groceries at the store.

Pretend play with language. Children use words to further their pretend stories. They may describe the imaginary action or tell other children how to play their roles.

Pretend play with others. Children play in a group of at least three or four other children.

Pretend play lasting at least ten minutes. After setting up for play, children play out the story line for at least ten minutes.

Time to Reflect

What do the children in your setting like to pretend? What roles do they use?

_____

_____

_____

_____

How Toys and Props Influence Play

Toys or props in your environment influence the types of play children choose. Children in a dramatic play area tend to play together in cooperative play, but the same children playing with playdough may engage in solitary or parallel play. Likewise, as children play with objects, you may see more pretend play in the dramatic play area and more constructive play in the block area. By including toys that encourage a variety of levels in play with others and object exploration, you give every child an opportunity to play. Think about what types of play, such as solitary play or sensorimotor play with objects, are encouraged through various play toys, activities, or learning areas in your learning environment and complete the chart using examples.

ENCOURAGING A VARIETY OF LEVELS IN PLAY

Play with Others	Toys, Activities, or Areas
Solitary Play	
Parallel Play	
Associative Play	
Cooperative Play	

Play with Objects	Toys, Activities, or Areas
Sensorimotor	
Constructive	
Dramatic	

The remaining chapters of this book help you create successful play experiences for children. Your support during play ranges from evaluating your environment and how it sustains children's play to creating interesting and exciting dramatic play themes based on your curriculum. Sometimes children have challenges playing together in a group. They may have ongoing conflicts or get stuck playing the same theme over and over and over. You can help children overcome these obstacles by your careful observation, problem solving, and planning. Aim to offer all children in your setting opportunities to imagine, communicate, pretend, and plan together during play.

Time to Reflect

Think about how children play with others as they first enter your group. How does their play change during the year as they get older and know each other better?

_____

_____

_____

_____

If two children were building towers in the block area, but not building together, how would you encourage them to connect with each other as they play?

_____

_____

_____

_____

Facilitating Dramatic Play CHAPTER 3

Your environment is the framework for children's play. You decide what children will play with, where they will play, and what adult roles they will reflect. In other words, you are arranging the space for play, providing the props and toys, and deciding how much time within your schedule you will put aside for play. Your decisions encourage imaginative play or dampen it. It can be a complicated role given the many variables influencing play. As you design your environment, consider your space, props, and materials, as well as the amount of time you provide in your schedule for play.

Content in this chapter connects with chapter 3 in *Play: The Pathway from Theory to Practice.*

Time to Reflect

What theme do you currently have for dramatic play in your learning environment? How do you see the children using the areas?

_____

_____

_____

_____

Providing Space for Dramatic Play

The following sections describe ways to improve children's play experiences through the arrangement of your space.

Keep the Area Well Defined, Enclosed, and Visible

Children tend to gravitate to spaces that are enclosed and set apart. When shelves provide the boundaries for the space, they seem to feel more secure. Perhaps they are not as concerned that someone will interrupt their play and will choose to play longer. However, you want the area to be visible so you can provide guidance and support when needed. Even though family child care providers may not have distinct learning areas, you can set aside a portion of your playroom for dramatic play with relevant props.

Ensure the Space Is the "Right" Size

The "right" size is sometimes difficult to determine. When a space is too large, children may engage in more running, wandering, and rough-and-tumble play. These activities can be disruptive in an indoor space with a variety of props and furniture. When a space is too small, children may fight, push, or argue more. Observe the children's play. If they are running, make your space smaller. If you notice fighting and conflicts while children are playing in your area, make the area larger. Although changing the space may not completely solve the issue, size could be a factor, and changing it is an easy way to support children's play.

Keep the House Area

Often teachers will change the dramatic play area to reflect a theme or unit they are exploring. For example, you may be discussing health for a few weeks. You might read books on health, play games about good nutrition, cook healthy food, and set up a doctor's office for a dramatic play area. When you set up the doctor's office, be sure to keep the house area as well, even if you make it smaller. Keeping the house area extends the play beyond the one theme. Children can be in the house area, have a sick baby, and go to the doctor's office. Then they can bring the baby home and feed him. Many children will continue to use the house area as a base because the themes in the house area are those they know best: cooking, eating, sleeping, and family relationships.

Put the House and Block Areas Close to Each Other

If the house area and block area are close to each other, children will have the opportunity to go back and forth between them to enrich their play. Children can leave the house area and go to the block area to get on a bus or train and then return home. Sometimes teachers are reluctant to let children take props from one area to another. This is understandable as things can become lost and the areas can become quite messy and disorganized. Cleanup can be a chore to complete. To keep the activity somewhat calmer, you can set limits on the kinds of props that can be moved around. For example, writing tools can be moved from the writing area to the house area, but paints must be used in the art area. Large blocks can be moved to a different area, but the steering wheel bench must remain in the block area.

Use Outdoor Space for Dramatic Play

Setting up dramatic play areas outside can bring a whole new set of players into the experience. Sometimes active children will be attracted to a larger space and a less restricted environment. Some themes to consider outside are car washes, washing baby clothes, shoe stores, and painting with water on a wall like an artist.

Time to Reflect

Describe your dramatic play space. Where is furniture placed?

_____

_____

_____

_____

Is the dramatic play area well defined, enclosed, and visible? Is the space the "right" size? Why or why not?

_____

_____

Do you keep the house area when you change the dramatic play theme? Why or why not?

_____

_____

Do you put the house area and the block area close to each other? Why or why not?

_____

_____

Do you provide space outdoors as well as indoors for dramatic play? Why or why not?

_____

_____

What questions do you have about dramatic play spaces?

_____

_____

_____

_____

Envision Your Space

Another way to understand space and how you arrange it is to draw your floor plan. You may see new ways of moving the areas around to encourage more concentrated play.

Drawing the Floor Plan

Draw the floor plan of your learning environment.

After drawing your floor plan, what do you notice?

_____

_____

_____

_____

How would you consider changing it in the future?

_____

_____

_____

_____

Providing Props and Materials

Props or toys determine the kinds and depths of play in your dramatic play area. Sometimes children will ask for certain toys to play out a theme, but most of the time you are the one who chooses props to include. You don't want to overwhelm children with too many props, but you also want to have enough. You want the props to line up with a theme. You want them to be appealing to children, yet also serve a learning purpose. The following are some considerations when you choose props for your dramatic play areas.

Consider the Stage of Play You Want to Encourage

Remember when you completed the Play with Objects chart in chapter 2? You saw that certain props encourage certain kinds of play. Playdough encourages solitary or parallel play. Blocks can encourage cooperative play, and a kitchen area can encourage sociodramatic play. For sociodramatic play, choose props that support interaction among the children and the use of pretend play.

Time to Reflect

Look at your dramatic play area again. What props have you included in the area? Which stages of play do these props encourage?

_____

_____

_____

_____

Have Enough Props to Involve Multiple Children

Judging how many props to offer often depends on the ages of the children. Three-year-olds may have more problems sharing than older children. Make sure you have more than one item so conflicts don't get in the way of play. When I (Sandy) was in graduate school, I was teaching three-year-olds in the therapeutic preschool. I noticed they were frequently fighting over a toy telephone. I started to devise a plan to help them share. However, my supervisor just suggested I get more than one phone. Although the answer seemed a little simple, I brought in more phones and the fighting lessened so the play wasn't disrupted by conflicts.

When an item is popular, it may draw more children. Sometimes you can't have enough for every child. In those cases, you can help children share by structuring turns. Children love to ride trikes, but programs cannot afford to have more than a few trikes. You can structure turns by making a list or using a timer. You will also need to decide when to put out props. Teachers often put out fewer props when they are setting up a new theme. After a couple of weeks, children can become a little restless. When you put out more and different props, children become reengaged.

Time to Reflect

Which toys are popular in your setting?

_____

_____

_____

_____

How do you help children take turns so every child has a chance to play with those toys?

_____

_____

_____

_____

Provide Real-Looking Objects and More Open-Ended Materials

Many of the props in your dramatic play area encourage pretend play. When a child lifts up a real-looking piece of fruit, she remembers the fruit from home or fruit shown in a book. Those real-looking props ground children in their pretend play because they reflect their experience. As children get older, they can pretend with objects that are more abstract and open-ended. A child may use a block as a piece of food on a plate or a group of blocks as a bed for the baby. You want to help children move to more abstract objects as they expand their imaginations.

Putting boxes or crates in the house area encourages children to use their imaginations as they decide what they want to use them for. If you add blankets they may create a house or another enclosure. Eventually children use imaginary objects to further their play. Children will pretend to give you money or food by just placing their hand on yours. You are expected to take the money or eat the food with relish. By varying the real-looking objects and more abstract objects in your dramatic play area, you give all children the opportunity to pretend at the level they are at and move them to more imaginary scenarios.

Time to Reflect

Look back at your list of dramatic play props. Put a star by the real-looking objects. List three props you could add to encourage more imaginary play.

_____

_____

_____

My doll was special, and I played "house" with tin doll dishes set up in one of the farm buildings that would be empty during the summer. Chunks of wood made chairs and table—a handkerchief for a tablecloth. Play included all the housekeeping kinds of chores and joys—pretending meals, doing dishes, doing laundry, and reading stories. —Justine

Include Early Literacy and Math Props

Children who encounter early literacy and math props will include them in their play and gain valuable knowledge about their use in real life. For example, children playing store can put prices on the food they are selling or list numbers on a sign. They can write or have written for them the names of the foods and then post them. To accomplish this they need to have paper and writing utensils in the area. Putting out advertising circulars gives them more ideas for using words and numbers. Including a play cash register increases their knowledge of numbers. When they use these words and numbers, they are incorporating what they see adults doing. They begin to understand the function of words and numbers and gain more motivation to learn them.

Below is a chart for you to complete. In one column are dramatic play themes. Write in early math and literacy props that relate to the theme. One example is included to get you started.

EARLY MATH AND LITERACY PROPS

Dramatic Play Theme	Early Math Props	Early Literacy Props
Shoe store	Cash register	Advertising flyers
House	Phone	Cookbook
Doctor's office	Thermometer	Appointment sheet
Pizza shop	Menu	Order pad
Camping	Map	List of equipment

Offer Props Related to a Theme

Children are drawn to dramatic play areas with a theme and props that reflect the theme. If you have a house area, you include a stove with pots and pans, a cupboard with dishes, a table and chairs, dolls and doll beds, baby clothes, and bottles. You may include plastic food, spoons to stir the food, and pretend boxes such as macaroni and cheese. If you decide to add a restaurant to the house area, you may add menus, order pads, a posted menu, aprons, and play pizzas and pizza boxes. These props help children develop the theme as they play together. They spark the children's ideas about what they could play and the roles children in the group could have. A restaurant theme needs customers, servers, cooks, and greeters. The props you provide give children clues about what to do and how to talk with one another. You can see how important props are to the development of children's play.

Time to Reflect

Choose a new dramatic play theme for your learning environment. List props you would like to include.

_____

_____

_____

_____

List some ways you could introduce those props. Include words you would use.

_____

_____

_____

_____

My grandpa sold insurance, and I used to beg my brother and cousins to play office with me. We would use old Sears/J.C. Penney catalogs, old telephones, and my grandpa's old day planners and calendars and take "orders" over the phone. —Sarah

Encourage Children to Explore and Engage

We know children act out roles they see around them, and objects become tools to develop the play scene. They love to play in the house area because they have all watched their parents cook and take care of them. But sometimes you may want to design a dramatic play area that is unfamiliar to some or all of the children. If you carefully plan how you introduce the new play area, children will be drawn to it.

However, if they do not understand how the props are used, they may spend their time just exploring how the objects work and not actually engage in dramatic play. You want the children to explore the objects but also to engage in pretend play. For example, let's say you want to set up a garden shop in the spring. Here are a few ways to help children understand this new theme:

- Go on a field trip to a garden shop.

- Read a book on gardening.

- Show children the props in large-group time and discuss how they are used.

- Show a video of planting a garden.

- Play with the children in the area after you have introduced it.

- Introduce a few props at first and then add more as the children become more experienced with the theme.

- Ask parents to talk about their experience with the theme.

- Plan and plant your own garden with the children either inside or outside.

The important piece of helping children learn new or unfamiliar dramatic play themes is to provide them with a variety of experiences, and you can do that in many ways.

Time to Reflect

What other ways could you introduce a new dramatic play theme to children?

_____

_____

Choose a child to observe during playtime. What do they do with the props and materials? Are they exploring them or pretending with them? If they are pretending, how do you know what they are pretending?

_____

_____

_____

_____

Providing Enough Time for Dramatic Play

Children need extended time to develop imaginative play scenarios. It takes time for children to explore props together, decide a play scenario, and organize the props, materials, and roles. Then they play together. If children don't have enough time, they may not even get beyond initial exploration of props. Children learn the most through play if it is developed fully. Researchers tell us children need at least thirty to forty minutes of extended time to fully develop a play scenario.

It is difficult to provide the full thirty to forty minutes for play at one time given the many demands on your schedule. Instead, you may allot fifteen minutes when children arrive and another fifteen minutes while waiting for lunch. Days are packed with activities, so you may feel discouraged when you hear how much time is needed for children's play. It may be a struggle to carve out time for play in your schedule while fitting in everything else, but children's play will become more complex and layered with the extended time.

Time to Reflect

Write down your daily schedule. How much time have you set aside for play? Is it all at one time or interspersed throughout the day?

_____

_____

_____

_____

What keeps you from setting aside enough time for play?

_____

_____

_____

_____

Teachers have shared some of the following challenges when making time for play:

- increasing demands for literacy and math activities
- short days with times already allotted for meals and snacks
- children's short attention spans
- planning around outside time and gym time with other teachers
- specialists' or consultants' visits

Although the demands are significant as you plan your daily schedule, here are some ideas to help you add more time for play:

- Combine smaller amounts of time designated for play into a larger amount of time.

- Shorten other activities such as large group or small group to extend time for play.

- Schedule specialists' visits at specific times.

- Hold playtime firm even when other demands are made on your schedule.

- Shorten other activities to make time for play.

- Set up dramatic play in a gym or outside.

- Encourage children to play the same dramatic play theme over a week or two.

Time to Reflect

What have you noticed about children's play when it is broken up into small periods of time?

_____

_____

_____

_____

What else could you do to add more extended time for play?

_____

_____

We played with Barbie dolls quite often. Mostly, we would set up buildings and houses (out of shoe boxes and furniture) and get them ready for things like fashion shows by spending hours choosing what they were going to wear. The Barbies rarely got to the actual "activity" that they planned for; it was usually just about getting them ready. —Lisa C.

Paying attention to your environment provides a backdrop for children's play in your setting. By setting up dramatic play areas with props related to the theme and providing enough extended time for play to develop, you help children's play skills deepen and mature.

Time to Reflect

After considering what you have read, choose at least one factor to change, such as enlarging or shrinking your dramatic play space, adding props, setting up a new dramatic play theme, or providing more time in the schedule devoted to play. Try the change for at least a week. What did you see children doing with the change? How did it influence their play?

_____

_____

_____

_____

Solving Problems CHAPTER 4

Whether problems occur in your personal life or in your work with children, how you address them reflects your childhood experiences, your personality, and what has worked for you in the past. For example, when I (Sandy) experience a problem, I worry about the problem at length and then try to fix it myself. I get anxious and want to solve it quickly. However, by trying to fix the problem before others have had the chance, I often come up with solutions that don't work. This is particularly true when working with children. I had to learn to step back and support children as they attempted to solve their own problems. When I did this, they were able to have the experience of making mistakes and learning from them. Here are some other ways you may address problems:

Content in this chapter connects with chapter 8 in *Play: The Pathway from Theory to Practice.*

- Avoiding: we look the other way and pretend it isn't happening.

- Blaming: we become angry with others and blame them for the problem.

- Self-blaming: we blame ourselves for the problem and may become depressed.

- Denying: we deny there is a problem when others point out the problem to us.

- Giving up: we decide there is nothing we can do and just stop trying to solve it.

- Solving the problem: we work with others to find solutions.

Some of these strategies do not lead to positive solutions. Denying the problem or giving up can make a bad situation worse. If you understand your approach to problem solving and you feel it is not productive for you, you can work to change it. The first step is to acknowledge and examine your approach.

Time to Reflect

Describe how you tend to react initially when you have a problem in your work with children.

_____

_____

_____

_____

Initial reactions may not always be the most helpful. Stepping back and thinking through your response may yield better results. How do you help yourself step back and think through a response?

_____

_____

_____

_____

☀ Mike knew he had a problem with the children in his group. Every day the cleanup took up to half an hour. During the choice time the children pulled almost every toy off the shelves and didn't put them back when they were finished. The floor in each area was filled with materials, toys, and props. When he gave the cleanup warning, the children ignored him and continued playing. The assistant teachers looked at each other and shook their heads. Mike just ignored his coworkers, concentrating on getting the children to clean up. But he knew they were right. He didn't know what to do. During cleanup the children often continued playing or fought with each other over the toys. He and the other staff often cleaned up by themselves. By the time the children got to large group, they were angry, restless, and hard to quiet. Mike was starting to resent the children and wondered if their parents let them act this way in their homes.

Time to Reflect

What was Mike's problem?

_____

_____

_____

_____

What was his reaction?

_____

_____

_____

_____

As you can see, Mike had several reactions to the problem of children not cleaning up when it was time. He ignored or avoided the other staff. He also avoided confronting the children by cleaning up himself. He was starting to blame the children and their parents. None of these reactions helped him step back, see the problem clearly, and find possible solutions. In fact, by avoiding and blaming, he was creating more resentment and conflict. Mike's response is easier to see because you are reading about it. It is much harder to see your own reactions to problems.

Time to Reflect

Think about a problem you had recently. It could be an issue with a coworker, parent, or child. Describe the problem.

_____

_____

_____

_____

What was your reaction?

_____

_____

_____

_____

Was this reaction typical?

_____

_____

_____

_____

Were you able to solve the problem?

_____

_____

_____

_____

Steps for Effective Problem Solving

Although you have your own ways of responding to problems that may work for you, you can learn even more effective problem-solving skills. Here are helpful problem-solving steps that lead to possible solutions:

1. **Identify the problem.** Identifying the problem may be difficult. It is hard to focus on just one issue because there are usually several issues going on. If you can focus on the main problem, it will be easier to come up with good solutions.

2. **Gather information.** You gather information by carefully evaluating how your environment is set up and by observing how the children are responding and how you react to them.

3. **Brainstorm solutions.** When you brainstorm, simply write down all your ideas even if they seem unworkable. You will not use all of the ideas, but thinking of them will help you think more creatively.

4. **Pick the best idea.** Use information about the interests of your children, what they like, your own comfort level, and suggestions of others to pick the best idea. Draw on your training, reading, and education to help you choose.

5. **Try it.** Try your idea, but not just once. Give it a chance for at least two to three weeks.

6. **Decide if it is working.** After you have given your solution a fair trial, observe and decide if your idea has worked. You will know things have improved when you see the problem happening much less.

7. **Revise if needed.** If the solution hasn't worked, choose another idea or change the plan a little. It is not a failure if it hasn't worked. You have learned information you can use as you brainstorm ideas. You have eliminated an idea that won't work right now. Don't give up. Persistence will pay off.

Let's recall Mike and his problem. What if Mike decided to follow these problem-solving steps? How would that look?

☀ Mike pulled out a piece of paper and wrote out his thoughts using the steps in problem solving.

1. **Identify the problem.** The children won't clean up. They don't stop playing when I ask them to and cleanup takes a long time.

2. **Gather information.** I observed the children and staff. The children pull all of the toys off the shelves and do not put them away when they are done with them. They love to play and have a hard time stopping when I ask them to. They ignore my cleanup warning, which I give to the whole group. Because of the turmoil during cleanup, children are restless and hard to settle when they come to group. The other staff and I clean up all the toys and are starting to resent each other and the children.

3. **Brainstorm solutions.** I met with the assistant teachers and first apologized for ignoring the cleanup problem for so long. I asked them to help me brainstorm solutions:
    -   Set a timer to let the children know it is cleanup time.
    -   Give the cleanup warning to each child or group of children.
    -   Teach them a cleanup song to sing together as they are cleaning up.
    -   Gather them together before cleanup starts and assign tasks.

- Show the children a toy and ask them to clean up all toys just like that one.
- Ask them to clean up toys as they are done with them.
- Help children clean up but not do all of the cleanup.
- Allow the children a little more time to play before starting cleanup.

4. **Pick the best idea.** I think the children would respond well to a cleanup song. I am going to teach them a cleanup song tomorrow and then use it every day. I will sing the song as a way to let them know it is cleanup time. I also will give the warning to individual children or groups of children rather than loudly letting the whole group know. I will try this for two weeks.

5. **Try it.** I tried this for two weeks. The children loved the song and started cleaning up right away.

6. **Decide if it is working.** Cleanup still takes too long. I have so much in my schedule to do, and I am almost spending more time cleaning up than letting children play.

7. **Revise if needed.** In addition to using the cleanup song, I am going to help children clean up as they are done with toys so there are not so many toys out when cleanup starts.

Time to Reflect

What do you think of Mike's problem-solving steps?

_____

_____

_____

_____

Are there other ideas you would try?

_____

_____

_____

_____

Shanita worked in a program serving children and their families experiencing severe stress. Many of the children had experienced neglect and abuse in their households. One child in particular, Cory, was hitting and kicking teachers on a regular basis. They tried several strategies, such as talking with him, separating him from the group, and giving him extra attention when he cooperated. However, the situation wasn't improving. Shanita and the other teachers met with their supervisor and designed a comprehensive support plan. The first day they tried the plan, Shanita grew more and more upset as the day went on. Cory continued to hit and kick the teachers even when they followed through with the new plan. After class, Shanita ran up to her supervisor in tears and exclaimed, "It didn't work. What are we going to do now?" Her supervisor looked surprised and then decided to meet with the team to discuss their reactions. After the supervisor listened to their discouragement and fears that Cory's behavior would never get better, she proposed trying the plan for two weeks before they decided it wasn't working. She explained they needed to give the plan time to work.

Keep Trying

When we try an idea, we want it to work right away, because often we have been living with the frustration and irritation for some time. But changing the circumstances that are causing a problem takes time, work, and persistence. Even if your idea is working, you may not see improvement right away. Sometimes children's behavior worsens before it gets better. As children discover their old ways of acting no longer work, they may try harder to make them work. But eventually you will see improvement as the problem lessens. Sometimes it won't be dramatic improvement, but it will be enough so you feel some relief. Sometimes you may even forget about the problem until you are reminded of it.

However, if your idea isn't working after giving it some time, you will need to revise it or try another idea. You might feel discouraged and want to give up. But keep at it. We often find our best ideas after first trying something that doesn't work. Effective problem solving requires good ideas and perseverance.

Perseverance

Angela Duckworth, an assistant professor at the University of Pennsylvania, wondered what qualities contributed to success in school. She has conducted several studies and concluded that perseverance—or grit—may contribute more to success than even IQ. People who were tenacious, stuck to the task, and showed backbone when confronted with challenging or discouraging situations were demonstrating grit. She found that people with grit were able to do better than others who were less likely to stick with a situation when it became hard.

When you are experiencing challenges with children in your group, your perseverance will eventually pay off. You may not see improvement immediately, but continuing to problem solve and experiment with your ideas will result in richer play experiences for all children in your group. Consider the following actions to help increase your perseverance:

- Set an achievable goal and pledge to reach it within a given time frame.

- Break down the goal into smaller steps.

- When you complete the smaller steps, share your accomplishment with a friend.

- If you become discouraged, reframe your experience to a more positive outlook.

- If you become distracted by a new play challenge, go back to your original goal before you take on the new one.

- When you've reached your goal, celebrate your achievement.

To learn more about Angela Duckworth and to complete her scale, go to https://sites.sas.upenn.edu/duckworth/pages/research.

Help from Others

Another way to increase your perseverance is to enlist the assistance of others. It is easier to stick with solving a problem if you are part of a group. Team members, parents, supervisors, friends, and other family child care providers can listen as you talk through your thoughts and help you think about solutions. Here are some ways to get help from others:

- Brainstorm with team members.

- Read about the problem and its possible solutions.

- Talk with other family child care providers.

- Consult with professionals from other disciplines, such as physical therapists, psychologists, and speech therapists.

Time to Reflect

What are some additional ways you can get help from others?

_____

_____

_____

_____

Who are your trusted confidants who listen to your concerns about your work and offer support?

_____

_____

_____

_____

These problem-solving steps give you the tools to address a variety of issues you see in your setting. Your willingness to examine your reactions honestly, brainstorm ideas, and choose a strategy helps you step back and think through what you want to accomplish. Although these steps can be used to respond to staff problems and address conflicts with parents, this book focuses on the kinds of challenges children experience while playing together. Your ability to problem solve these kinds of challenges opens up opportunities for children.

You play a central role in helping children engage in play, solve conflicts and learn to play peacefully together. Your thoughtful consideration of your role becomes part of the bigger plan. Sometimes your role involves setting the conditions for play, such as rearranging the environment or changing dramatic play themes. At other times you will play a more direct role, such as entering play or introducing children to the problem-solving steps. It will depend on what you see as the problem and what the children need to support them.

You also have a role as an evaluator. When you try out a strategy, you evaluate whether it is working or not. If not, you go to another strategy until you find a solution. Your careful observation skills help you understand how your strategy is affecting the children and whether your idea is helping the children move toward more mature play skills.

Use the problem-solving steps when you experience issues with the children in your group to give you a way to step back, think of possible options, and choose a viable action to solve the issue. Include a consideration of your role in solving the problem. Remember to keep trying if it doesn't work the first time. Your perseverance will pay off.

Time to Reflect

Write down your reflections after you read the paragraph above. After reading this, I am thinking about the following:

_____

_____

_____

_____

Negotiating Play Conflicts CHAPTER 5

It is not unusual for groups of children to have conflicts while playing together. Conflicts often erupt over sharing toys, taking turns, and feeling left out. Sometimes you may not be able to tell what children are fighting about. Conflicts can try the patience of adults working with them, especially if the fights occur again and again over the same issue. Adults may want to settle the conflicts so they can get to the real work of teaching. However, when adults use conflict in play to teach children how to handle disagreements and solve problems, they are teaching children a skill for life. It is worth spending the time to help children figure out things.

Content in this chapter connects with chapters 3 and 8 in *Play: The Pathway from Theory to Practice*.

Time to Reflect

Think of a time when a group of children was not playing well together in your dramatic play area.

Describe what they were doing.

_____

_____

_____

_____

How did you feel?

_____

_____

_____

_____

What did you do about it?

_____

_____

_____

_____

☀ It was the first day of school and Li was excited. She had worked all week to get ready. She had divided the room into learning areas, added math and literacy props to her dramatic play area, and placed labels around the room. The children were excited too. They played in all the areas and were quiet and focused in their play. Li felt confident, as if she really could do this teaching thing. Within two to three months, however, she was frustrated. Several children in her class played in the house area every day and often fought with each other over who would be the dad, who would get to cook, and what the mom would say. Li felt like she had tried everything. Sometimes she sat and talked with them. Other times, she broke the group up and told them to play somewhere else. But the next day the group would start fighting all over again. Li didn't know what to do and felt like just giving up.

Understanding Children in Conflict

Previous chapters explored how to set up your environment to encourage more imaginative play. But even with a well-set-up environment, children cannot always agree. They have conflicts over toys, roles, or turns. Like Li, we imagine what children's play will look like when we set up the dramatic play area. In our imaginations we see groups of children playing house together, acting out the roles of mom, dad, baby, and sister. We see them cooking together, setting the table, eating, and holding the baby. We put out dress-up clothes for them and envision how cute they will look in the jackets and aprons.

However, when children fight it is easy to feel discouraged or frustrated. Learning to put those feelings aside, brainstorming possible actions, and finding ways to get through these challenges to help children gain more successful and mature play skills are all part of learning to be an effective and intentional teacher.

Why Conflict during Play Is a Problem

Any time children play together there are opportunities for conflict. As they play, they form friendships. Conflict between friends is natural, and learning to solve conflicts successfully will strengthen relationships. But if conflict is allowed to fester, occurs frequently, or scapegoats certain children, it will erupt over and over again. Although conflict is distressing for those directly involved, it also affects the whole group. Children observing the fight, especially if it occurs often, may become anxious. It may seem like no one knows what to do, and the situation may feel out of control.

☀ Markus, Sammy, and Derek were fighting again. Tonya, the family child care provider, sighed and walked over to the boys. They fought every day over who was going to play with a special block. It was shaped like a cone and was fun to haul around in trucks and carry in backpacks. Sometimes they would raise their voices as they argued, but other times—like today—they were pushing and hitting each other. She felt like she had tried everything to get them to stop. She had separated them, scolded them, and set up turns, and yet every day, here they were again, fighting over the same toy. She was so frustrated she was ready just to remove it from the play area.

Time to Reflect

If Tonya came to you for help, what would you tell her?

_____

_____

_____

_____

Reasons Children Fight

You have probably noted all kinds of conflicts children have during play. The boys in our example were fighting over a desired toy. Other conflicts happen over who gets to play. Here are some reasons children fight:

- They fight over toys and props: some toys are especially popular, such as certain dolls or trucks.
- They fight over roles in play: all the children in the group want to be doctors.
- They fight over who gets to play in the group: some children may be excluded.
- They fight over how many children get to play in the group: only three or four children can play because that is how many props are available.
- They fight over space: they want more room when building structures.
- They fight over play ideas: one child wants to play fire station and another wants to play space rockets.

To understand the reasons children are fighting and gain insight into solutions, you have to observe carefully. Ask yourself, "Who is fighting?" and "What are they fighting over?"

What You Might See When Children Are in Conflict

You usually cannot ignore children's conflicts. Their responses to conflict can be quite dramatic. You may see some or all of the following behaviors:

- raised voices
- pushing and shoving
- grabbing toys away
- excluding children
- crying
- angry faces

These behaviors indicate how stressful conflict can be for children and how much emotional energy it takes for you to help children with it.

Time to Reflect

Sometimes you know a conflict is going to happen before it starts. How can you tell when a conflict may occur? Think about what children fight over, where it may occur, and which children may be involved.

_____

_____

_____

_____

Your Reaction to Conflict

Children are not the only ones distressed by conflict. Adults are as well. If there are several adults in the room, each of them could have their own response to conflicts between children. Here are some possible reactions:

- anger toward the children
- resentment toward one child an adult believes is causing the conflict
- annoyance with the other adults for not solving the problem
- sadness

- fear for the safety of other children

- happiness that a shy child was standing up for himself

- confusion that the conflict continues to happen

Unsolved conflicts between children can bring up your own unsolved conflicts. Being aware of your feelings and putting them aside can help you come up with better ideas to solve children's conflicts. Talking through these feelings with your coworkers will help the team work together to come up with those best ideas.

Time to Reflect

Complete these sentences:

I feel good about conflict when

_____

_____

_____

_____

I hate conflict when

_____

_____

_____

_____

I've been reminded that I had frequent conflicts with my special friend Nikki. I'm afraid her brother Matt and I probably ganged up on her a lot, which wasn't very nice. I'm also pretty sure that I was really bossy toward her. I don't remember how we solved our conflicts. I think we probably went our separate ways and just eventually got over it, as kids do. I also probably tattled a lot, because from what I've heard about myself as a child that seems like something I would have done. I probably owe her a lot of apologies. —Sherry

Terri had a very active morning class. The children were constantly in conflicts with each other because they wanted the same toys, bumped into each other as they ran to the learning areas, and knocked down each other's block buildings. Terri found a book at the library called *No Fighting, No Biting!* written in 1958 by Else Holmelund Minarik. Terri was in a hurry and picked it up quickly. It sounded like something that might help her class. As she prepared for her group time, she found it had way too many words for her preschoolers and she almost didn't read it. However, she didn't have another story for the morning group so she decided to read part of it during her large-group time. In the book there are two little alligators named Quick-foot and Light-foot who are always fighting. Their mother tells them over and over again, "No fighting, no biting." The children listened quietly to the story and giggled whenever the alligators' mother said, "No fighting, no biting." Later that week Terri heard children fighting over who was going to set the table in the house area. She started to go over to help them, but then she heard the words "No fighting, no biting." The fighting stopped as other children helped them figure it out. For the rest of the year, children used the alligator mom's words to remind their friends to stop fighting. These words of advice didn't solve all of the conflicts, but it did remind children to find other ways of solving their problems with each other.

Using a Problem-Solving Approach

Another idea to consider is to try the same problem-solving steps you learned with the children. Children can learn to be good problem solvers if given the chance. However, when you problem solve with children, you have to put aside time to talk with them. You cannot be distracted or in a hurry because children need time to consider their options. Often they are upset and angry and need to explore their feelings before they are ready to talk about possible solutions. Here's an explanation of the problem-solving model used with children:

1. **Identify the problem.** Ask the children to stop fighting and to sit with you. Get down to their level and ask them what the problem is. At first children may blame the others and start another round of fighting. But calmly ask them again to tell you the problem. Restate the problem as they tell you. It could be something like, "You all want to have the new doll," or "Maria wants to play house and Tala wants to play school."

2. **Gather information.** Ask the children what happened while they were fighting. You will likely hear about hurt feelings, angry words, and perhaps physical fighting.

3. **Brainstorm solutions.** Ask them how they think they could solve this problem. Let them come up with a few ideas if they can. Add some of your ideas. Ask them to think about the ideas and how they would work. It may take some time, but try to move them to one idea.

4. **Pick the best idea.** Get agreement from all of the children involved in the conflict on the idea to try.

5. **Try it.** Try the idea, but not just once. Give it a chance for at least two to three weeks.

6. **Decide if it is working.** Check in with the children later to see if the idea is working.

7. **Revise if needed.** If the children decide it isn't working, ask if they have other ideas. Offer your own if they can't think of any.

Although going through the problem-solving steps with children can be time consuming, the gains for children are countless. They learn they can find ways to solve their conflicts without fighting. They learn they can have some control over their solutions, and they feel very good about themselves.

Time to Reflect

Describe a time you helped two children solve their conflict with each other.

_____

_____

_____

_____

How did the children feel about the solution and did the problem recur?

_____

_____

_____

_____

If the problem did happen again, what did you do?

_____

_____

_____

_____

Helping Solve Conflicts

Children often fight over valued toys, books, or activities. Consider the example of the children fighting over the cone-shaped block. Here are some possible solutions for this particular problem:

- Get more than one of the desired toy.
- Build a play theme around the cone, such as road construction.
- Ask children to play roles in the new play theme.
- Use a timer to arrange turns.

Time to Reflect

Which idea would you try? Why?

_____

_____

_____

_____

Do you have any additional ideas?

_____

_____

_____

_____

Here are more ideas for helping children solve conflicts about roles, props, or space during play:

- Help children play out themes by including props that give them many clues about the roles.

- Help children choose roles, especially when one role is highly desired, such as a mom or dad. Arrange turns if they can't agree on a compromise.

- Remind them they can create as many roles as they want for their group. Show how there can be more than one doctor, nurse, or mom.

- Offer to get more props if children are excluding other children because they don't have enough of a certain prop.

- Help children arrange space for building in the block area. Use tape or other means to define areas if needed.

- Enter the play to help children arrange roles and the play theme.

- Encourage them to ask you for help before they get mad at each other.

I usually solved problems with my friends without asking grown-ups for help. For example, my two younger cousins were having an argument, and me and my other cousin decided we would set up a court using a meat tenderizer as a gavel. We acted as the judge, heard the testimony from each girl, and came up with a ruling. Because we were a few years older, they listened to our ruling and did as we asked. I think the official ruling was that they had to apologize and give each other a hug. —Lisa C.

You can count on negotiating conflicts between young children when they are engaged in dramatic play. Children disagree about play scenes, who gets to play with the props, and which roles children will get to play. Help them learn how to listen when someone else is upset and express their thoughts about solutions. Give them the practice and time to learn these valuable skills, which they will carry with them for life.

Time to Reflect

Complete the following sentences:

The children in my class fight over

_____

_____

When they fight I feel like

_____

_____

The next time they fight I am going to

_____

_____

CHAPTER 6 # Helping Children Engage in Dramatic Play

Sometimes children just can't seem to engage in play with each other. They may wander around the room or avoid certain areas. Other times they may repeat the same play theme over and over until it seems stale. When children aren't engaged, they don't have the opportunities to develop their play skills. They may not connect to other children and eventually may cause trouble by running and tussling.

☀ Luis noticed that children were not engaging in the dramatic play area. They would either avoid the area, or if they did enter, they would go in, manipulate some objects, and then leave. Early in the year he set up a house area with a table and chairs, stove, refrigerator, and some dishes. He put a few dolls in there as well. Children went into the area and played with the dishes and dolls but didn't seem to be acting out roles, so Luis decided to change it. He wanted the play to be more complex and engaging. He took out the house area and put in a doctor's office. The girls in his class came in a little, but it still wasn't a big draw. They looked at the X-rays, checked out the bandages, and then left to play somewhere else. He had never had a class that seemed to avoid the dramatic play area. He thought introducing the doctor's office would help.

> ## Time to Reflect
>
> Put yourself in Luis's place. How would you react, especially when the new dramatic play area was not being used for play?
>
> _____
>
> _____
>
> _____
>
> _____

Content in this chapter connects with chapters 3 and 8 in *Play: The Pathway from Theory to Practice.*

Why Dramatic Play Avoidance Is a Problem

When children avoid the dramatic play area or play there for short periods of time, they don't have opportunities for the deep play that supports growth and development. The children in Luis's classroom were already having some difficulty with adopting and enacting roles and extending the play theme. But when he removed the house area and put in the doctor's office, children started by exploring the props rather than pretending with them. They weren't developing their play skills.

Reasons Children Avoid Dramatic Play

There are several possibilities to consider when children are not really engaging in the dramatic play area:

- The children may have shorter attention spans.
- The children may not understand the theme.
- The children may not be familiar with the props or understand how to use them.
- The children may not know each other well.
- The children may not have the play skills to develop the themes.

Time to Reflect

When you think about the children in Luis's room, why do you think they weren't engaging in either the house area or the doctor's office?

_____

_____

_____

_____

What You Might See If Children Are Avoiding Dramatic Play

Children are in the dramatic play area, but they are not playing out roles or talking about their pretend scenarios. They may look as if they are bored and need more interesting activities. But if teachers think children are bored, and misread the children's signals, they will add materials rather than help children learn to play together in a pretend scenario. Boredom and lack of engagement may look very similar, but you have to use your observations and knowledge of your group to make a determination. Here are some ways to tell if children are not engaged in the dramatic play theme:

- Children are going into the area and just looking at the props.
- Children are going into the area for a short time and leaving.
- Children are following others into the area but leaving quickly.
- Children are manipulating the props but not pretending with them.

Helping Children Engage in Dramatic Play

When Luis changed the dramatic play area to a doctor's office, he probably thought he would attract children to the area because it was something new. However, he may have skipped some steps that would have made his dramatic play area more successful and attractive to the children. Chapter 3 explored several ideas Luis could try to create more engaging dramatic play experiences:

- Keep the house area when introducing a new area. It gives the children a base from which to come and go.
- If the children have a short attention span for play activities, include sensorimotor material in the dramatic play theme. For example, use water when washing babies or playdough when cooking. This draws children to the area and keeps them there while they explore role-play activities.
- Introduce a new dramatic play theme by providing experiences. This could be through books, field trips, discussions, or other kinds of media, such as videos.
- Introduce a new dramatic play theme in large-group time before opening the area. Show children the props and talk about how they are used.
- Keep the play area in your learning environment long enough so that children can develop the theme.
- Enter play yourself, especially in the beginning, to help children understand the roles they could play.

Time to Reflect

When you read the preceding list, what do you think you would do to help children engage in the dramatic play area?

_____

_____

_____

_____

Looking at Dramatic Play Themes

Part of keeping children engaged in play is planning interesting dramatic play areas. When dramatic play areas reflect your learning projects, children practice their new understandings through play. Let's look at dramatic play themes a little more closely.

Incorporate At Least Four to Six Dramatic Play Areas a Year

The new dramatic play areas could reflect your learning units or themes, or they could emerge out of the children's interests. Some teachers create dramatic play areas from books they have been reading with the children. By changing the dramatic play area at least four to six times a year, you keep it interesting for the children and also give them time to develop roles and story lines around the new theme. Try to keep some of the house area as well as the new theme. Maybe you don't have enough space in your room to have a complete house area as well as another dramatic play theme, but modify your house area by pulling out just some of the furniture and props. Even a smaller house area will encourage more play between the two areas and help children with less mature play skills join in. Children with less mature play skills know about role-playing mothers, fathers, and babies, but they may not have the skills or experience to develop another kind of story line, such as camping or fishing, with other children.

Time to Reflect

What is your current learning unit, theme, or study?

_____

_____

Describe a dramatic play theme related to the unit. Include props and roles.

_____

_____

_____

_____

Choose Familiar Dramatic Play Themes

Dramatic play themes are most successful when children have had some experience with them. Children love to play what they have seen adults do. Dramatic play themes such as house areas, school, doctor's office, and stores are very popular. Think about the cultural backgrounds of the children in your group. What dramatic play themes reflect their neighborhoods or homes? What props could you include that reflect their cultures? For example, if you are setting up a store, be sure to include boxes with labels in languages the families speak. Children's play is richer if the props are familiar to them. You can set up play themes outside such as farming, car washes, and laundromats. You can also plan dramatic play areas based on books you have read or projects you are studying. Children can learn about less familiar themes through field trips, books, videos, and invited guests. Ask yourself these questions as you consider themes:

- What experiences have children had in their families and communities?
- What do families enjoy doing together?
- Are there cultural practices that could be included?
- Are there books they particularly like?
- Is there a project or study that could include a dramatic play theme?

Allow for Spontaneity

Always be ready for a spontaneous play theme that may emerge from the children's experience. In one classroom, the children started playing wedding. The leader of the play, a four-year-old girl, must have just gone to a wedding because she knew of many wedding traditions. The literacy mentor used the opportunity to talk about invitations and a map to get to the wedding. The children took the chairs by the tables and placed them in rows. The leader of the wedding play chose the groom and, of course, she was the bride. She found a dress and heels in the dress-up corner. Soon all the children in the group were playing along. The children sang as she walked down the aisle. To play this theme, the children simply used what they had around them and transformed it into a beautiful wedding. The children were very excited about this play theme and continued playing wedding for several days.

> In some ways, play hasn't changed that much. Kids still like to "play" what they
> see the grown-ups around them doing on a daily basis, whatever that may be.
> —Carrie

Time to Reflect

Imagine you live in an area with winter sports and decide to set up a new dramatic play theme for ice fishing. List the props you could include.

_____

_____

_____

_____

What additional props could you include to develop early literacy and early math skills?

_____

_____

Repetitive Dramatic Play

Sometimes children seem stuck playing the same theme over and over again. The roles and the story line remain the same every day. They may exclude other children who have not been part of the scenario. This pattern looks different from a lack of engagement, although gradually you may notice that the children seem a bit bored or restless. Mainly they are engaged but are repeating pretend actions, words, and roles in more of a rote fashion. By making a few changes, you can expand their play experiences and fully engage them again.

☀ Markus, Ian, and David ran into the block area, just like they did the day before and the day before that. They had played like this every day for three weeks. They laughed and pulled blocks down. They placed them side by side and straddled them. They moved their hands a little and made a motor sound with their mouths. It was clear they were pretending to ride motorcycles. When other children wanted to join them, they would tell them they couldn't play. The three boys would play like this the entire play period until it was time to clean up. Although they seemed to enjoy their daily motorcycle rides, there was little variation in their play. Maria, their teacher, was feeling a little impatient because the play was so repetitive, but she was also puzzled about what to do.

Time to Reflect

What are your thoughts when you read this example?

_____

_____

_____

_____

If you were Maria, what would be your reaction?

_____

_____

_____

_____

Why Repetitive Play Is a Problem

In some ways, the repetitive motorcycle play may not be causing a big problem. It could be easy to ignore, especially if other children are having ongoing conflicts or running around the room. We want children to gain the most they can from play, but this small group of children is not realizing this gain. The three boys are stuck, unable to vary their roles or language beyond the actual riding of the motorcycles. They are not designing other construction projects in the block area beyond setting up the motorcycles. Although they clearly enjoy each other's company, their friendship is mainly limited to this play scenario. Right now they are repeating the motorcycle play every day, but they could get bored and wander off, losing the possibility of forming deeper friendships. Their play is also affecting the other children, because they won't let anyone else play with them.

Time to Reflect

Do you agree or disagree with the preceding paragraph? Why or why not?

_____

_____

_____

_____

Reasons Children Become Stuck in a Play Theme

It can be hard to understand what children are pretending or exactly what story they are telling in their play. We try to interpret the pretend sequence by observing their language and actions. When we try to understand the reasons children may become stuck in a play theme, like motorcycle play, we are speculating. Here are some possible reasons children don't vary their play scenario:

- Children don't know various actions of the role of the motorcycle rider. They have seen others ride motorcycles, perhaps adults close to them, but they aren't aware of anything else motorcycle riders do.

- Children don't understand broader themes, such as transportation or community workers, and how their play may fit into them.

- Children don't have enough props to develop the theme further.

- The children have fun together, but none of them take the leadership to develop the play scenario.

- Children have some language difficulties, so they don't go beyond making the motor sounds.

What You Might See When Children Are Stuck in Repetitive Play

When children are repeating a theme over and over, it becomes a pattern. This pattern helps us predict what may happen next. For example, the three boys pulled down the blocks every day and sat on them. After a few days you would be able to predict what they would do when it was time to play. These behaviors demonstrate how stuck they are. You may see one or more of the following behaviors:

- The scenario is one-dimensional and focuses on one theme or one role without variation.

- The play is repetitive, with children engaging in the same actions over and over again.

- The language or sounds they use don't change.

- The engagement level is low and children may act bored, wander off quickly, or don't seem involved in creating new avenues to explore in play.

Your Reaction to Repetitive Play

Explore your reactions when you notice children's play challenges. Your initial reactions can block creative brainstorming and stop you from seeing the issue in a more objective fashion. Start by acknowledging what you are feeling. Remember that Maria, the teacher in the scenario, felt both impatient and puzzled about what to do. She could choose to ignore the three boys' play, because it isn't causing big problems in her class. If she doesn't grapple with it, however, the children will have lost an opportunity for growth. If Maria understands her initial responses and decides to address the repetitive motorcycle play, she becomes more intentional about how she sets up her block area and how she interacts with the children.

Here's another example of children stuck in a play theme. After you read it, complete the first four steps of the problem-solving approach.

☀ Candace had set up a grocery store two weeks ago in her dramatic play area. She set it up next to the house area. She included boxes, cans, and pretend food on the shelves, a cash register on the counter, and a play grocery cart. The same four children went there every day. They put the boxes in the grocery cart and rolled the cart around. They ignored the cash register and didn't play any roles. Candace felt disappointed that the children weren't fully using the grocery store.

Time to Reflect

Identify the problem. What is the problem?

_____

_____

_____

_____

Gather information. What do you see happening?

_____

_____

_____

_____

Brainstorm solutions. What are your ideas?

_____

_____

_____

_____

Pick the best idea. What would work best given your group of children?

_____

_____

_____

_____

Broadening Play Scenarios

When children are stuck in a play theme, your goal will be to broaden their play scenario. Think about the three boys riding the motorcycles. You could broaden this theme by:

- adding theme-related props, such as helmets, gloves, tools, road signs, buildings to visit, or backpacks for the children to carry.

- suggesting further theme development, such as a repair shop to fix the motorcycles.

- playing a role with them, such as a police officer directing traffic or a mechanic at the repair shop.

- asking other children to play roles in the expanded theme, such as the police officer or the mechanic.

- planning roles that don't use a lot of language, such as fixing the motorcycles.

Time to Reflect

What would you do to broaden the motorcycle play?

_____

_____

_____

_____

When teachers are frustrated or impatient about children's group play, they may try ideas that work in the short-term but do not provide a longer-term solution. Some teachers will close the area. They may limit the time the children can play in the area. They may insist that other children have to be included. None of these are bad ideas per se, but they do not help reach the goal of broadening the play theme. Going back to the motorcycle example, you will be more successful if you use the boys' interests and friendship. The three boys obviously enjoy playing together. By building on that rather than trying to control it, you help them develop their friendship, interests, and play skills. If new roles are introduced, they may naturally include other children.

Time to Reflect

Have you ever closed a learning area because the children weren't using it well? What were the children doing? How did this strategy work?

_____

_____

_____

_____

Using a Decision Tree

Another way to settle on the best idea is to use a decision tree. By asking a set of questions you may be able to determine more information about the problem and reach a reasonable solution.

The following is an example of a decision tree you could use to select the best action when children are playing repetitively.

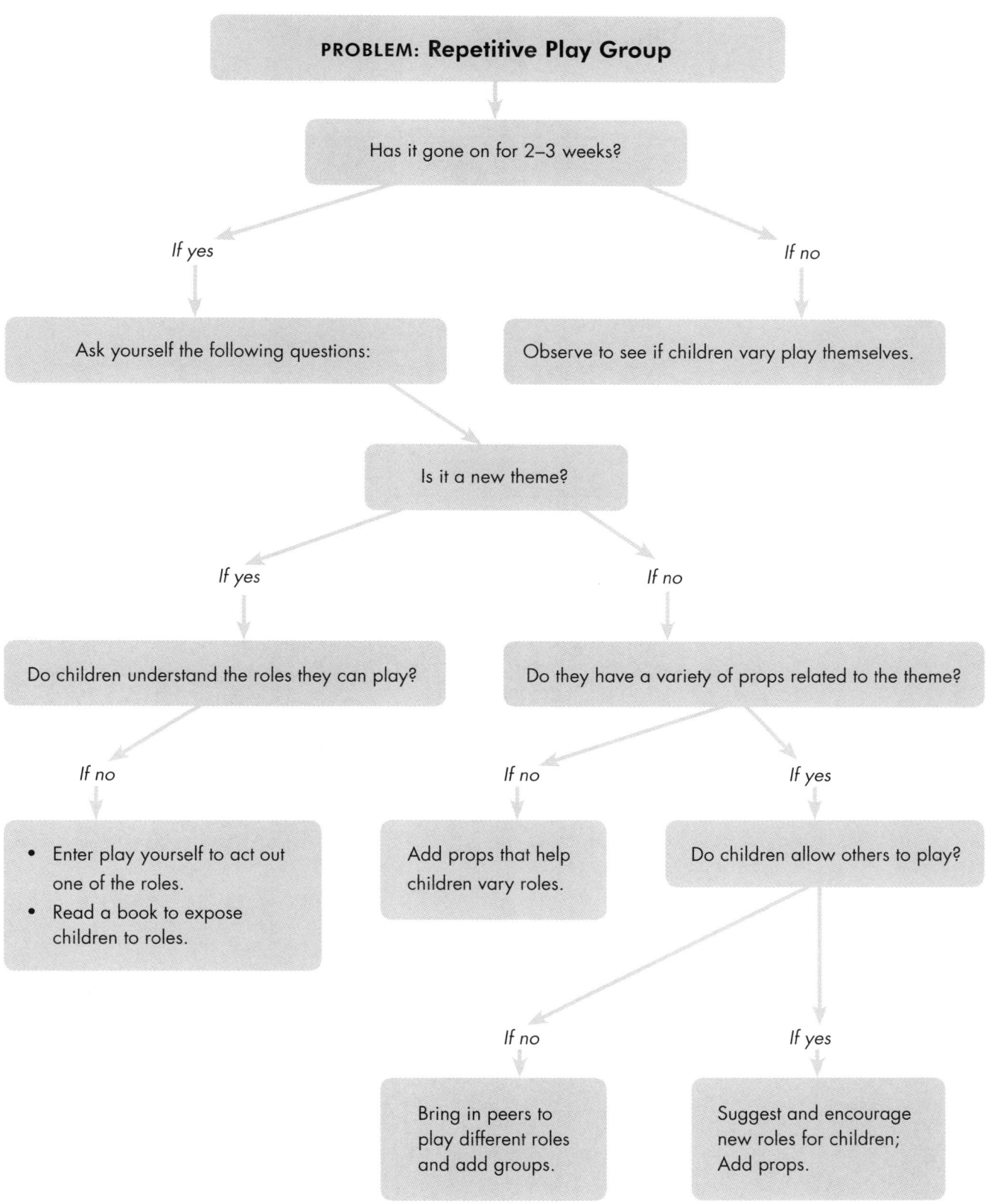

PROBLEM: Repetitive Play Group

Has it gone on for 2–3 weeks?

If yes

Ask yourself the following questions:

If no

Observe to see if children vary play themselves.

Is it a new theme?

If yes

Do children understand the roles they can play?

If no

Do they have a variety of props related to the theme?

If no

- Enter play yourself to act out one of the roles.
- Read a book to expose children to roles.

If no

Add props that help children vary roles.

If yes

Do children allow others to play?

If no

Bring in peers to play different roles and add groups.

If yes

Suggest and encourage new roles for children; Add props.

Time to Reflect

What are your questions as you read through the decision tree?

_____

_____

_____

_____

Would this method of problem solving be helpful to you? Why or why not?

_____

_____

_____

_____

Children show a lack of engagement in play when they wander around the room or only explore the props you provide in the dramatic play rather than pretend with them. Children may get stuck playing a play theme over and over without variation. In both situations, children will benefit from strategies designed to move them into more engagement and pretend play.

Responding to Physical or Violent Play Themes

Children love to wrestle, push each other in fun, and run around with abandon. Sometimes their play reflects the violence they have seen around them, whether from television, movies, or in their own neighborhoods. The content of the play can be disturbing, but even if it is not, the play can quickly spiral out of control. Teachers often react by limiting the type of play children can engage in. They forbid guns even when they are constructed of Lego blocks. They ask children to stop roughhousing, particularly during play indoors. Some limits are needed to ensure everyone's safety. But children seem to be drawn to these themes and experiences, and if you stop to observe and analyze this attraction, you may find ways to use that interest to engage children further in play.

Content in this chapter connects with chapters 3 and 8 in *Play: The Pathway from Theory to Practice.*

※ Darius and Sydney were playing in the house area. All of a sudden, Olivia, the teacher, noticed they were both carrying blocks and creeping around the furniture in that area. She walked over and listened while they discussed hearing a robber in the house and how they had to get him. They stood up quickly and pretended they were shooting a girl who was cooking at the stove. The child they shot at turned around with wide eyes and started to cry. The two boys took their blocks and walked over to the block corner, looking for the robber. Olivia stopped them and told them they couldn't play guns in the classroom. She pointed out that their friend was still crying by the stove. Darius and Sydney looked over at her, surprised. Olivia took them over to the girl and asked them to talk with her. The boys excitedly told the girl they were just trying to get the robber who was in the house. They patted her on the arm. After that interaction, Olivia asked them to put the blocks away and took them to the writing center for another activity.

Time to Reflect

What violent themes have you seen children play?

_____

_____

_____

_____

What is your reaction when children play in violent ways?

_____

_____

_____

_____

Why Violent Play Is a Problem

Violent play may be very disturbing for you. Many of us remember playing cops and robbers, war, or some other form of violent play as we grew up. This play often reflected what we saw on television and at the movies. Children today also act out violent scenes they see in their lives. Experts are concerned, however, because the violence seems more persistent and reflects darker themes in the media as well as the violence they see in their homes or communities. Children get focused on the violence they see and hear and can't seem to move beyond the guns, bombs, and fighting. In a learning environment, violent play can be loud, escalate into fighting, and increase anxiety and excitement. It is no wonder many teachers would like to stop it quickly.

Time to Reflect

What are your concerns when children are acting out violent themes as they play?

_____

_____

_____

_____

Reasons Children Engage in Violent Play

The reasons children play violently are complex and multilayered. There is no single reason. Looking at various reasons, however, helps us understand why children can be so intense and focused when enacting violent themes in their play. Sometimes you may have to stop the violent play because it becomes too disruptive. But other times you could try to redirect it to capture the intense focus and interest. Here are some reasons for children's violent play:

Children see violence on television, in movies, and in video games. Although they say they want to see it, it can also make them anxious and fearful. This anxiety contributes to the intensity of their play. Violence is a common theme in the media, and children are frequently exposed to it.

Children may see violence in their families and in their neighborhoods. When violence touches children directly, they become very anxious and fearful. They may act out by becoming angry and violent. Violent themes are often a way for them to gain some mastery over a traumatic event.

Children may think violence is a way to solve problems. People get other people to do what they want by threatening violence. Children may get the toy they want by threatening or hitting other children.

Children enact violent themes to combat feelings of powerlessness. They may feel decisions that affect them are out of their control. Playing with weapons, capturing robbers, or playing soldiers helps them feel more powerful.

Time to Reflect

Why do you think children play violently?

_____

_____

_____

_____

Write about a child in your room who frequently wants to pretend play with weapons. Why do you think this is so?

_____

_____

_____

_____

What You Might See When Children Enact Violent Play

Children engaged in violent play are easy to spot:

- Children may carry and pretend to use guns, knives, and bombs.
- Children will make noises to go along with the weapons.
- Children may try to be secretive about weapon play, especially if you have a rule of "No Guns."

- Children will pretend to shoot each other or stab another child with a pretend knife.
- Children may pretend the toy dinosaurs or animals in the block area are fighting each other.
- Children use play cars in chase and crash scenes during play.
- Children may threaten violence as they play.
- Children may use inappropriate language.

Time to Reflect

What are some other behaviors you've observed during children's violent play?

_____

_____

_____

_____

☀ Tyrone, like many other children at his therapeutic preschool, received individual play sessions to help him deal with the trauma in his life. It was an opportunity for him to use play to gain mastery over trauma. Because so many of the children had been exposed to guns, the play session room had play guns available to the children. The classrooms did not. The children accepted the difference in rules after the teachers and play therapists explained it. Tyrone had been caught in a drug raid at his house and had seen his parents handcuffed and thrown on the floor. When it was time for his play session, he entered the room and ordered the play therapist on the floor. He pretended to handcuff her. He pretended to shoot at all of the pictures on the wall. He threatened her with a toy gun. He searched the room by overturning the buckets of toys. The play therapist continued to talk about how scary it must have been. Eventually he stopped the gun play and went to the puzzles. He sat calmly with the play therapist and completed several puzzles. Although Tyrone played out this scene a few more times, it was never with the intensity of the first time. His first reenactment of the drug raid seemed to relieve much of his anxiety.

Addressing Violent Play

Addressing violent play is challenging on many levels for teachers. It can bring up intense feelings for the children as well as for the adults. Sometimes the techniques you try don't work quickly, and the play continues to be violent. The ways to address it will vary depending on your situation, the children, and their families. The following strategies include ideas to try during play as well as at other times in the day.

Monitor props. Even though you do not allow play guns, children will make them. They will use blocks, manipulatives, and sticks as pretend guns. It often doesn't work when you completely ban guns. However, if you tell them not to make guns, discuss why. Use part of your large-group time to talk about how you want your group to be peaceful. Emphasize that guns are scary and that you want everyone to feel safe in the group. Some children may see guns at home. Emphasize that guns should be locked up and used only by adults because they can hurt people. Remind children never to touch a gun and to tell an adult if they see one.

Encourage children to express their feelings about the violence they are witnessing. Whether it is on television or in person, children should be encouraged to talk about their feelings. They may get excited and anxious while they are talking, but it is better for them to talk about it than to play it out violently. Ask them to draw pictures and then talk about them.

Read books about peace and solving conflicts. Show the children that there are better ways to solve problems than through violence. Tell stories, act out plays, and discuss other ways to solve conflict. (See chapter 5 for more information on negotiating play conflicts.)

Redirect the play so it reflects the children's ideas, yet brings it away from the violent theme. When Darius and Sydney were looking for the robbers in the house area, Olivia asked them to stop and took them to another area. What if she had thought about another way for them to play out this theme? Perhaps Darius and Sydney could pretend they were police officers (without guns) and were protecting the girl in the house. They could wear police hats and use a pretend cell phone. This theme could branch out into others, such as providing medical attention (someone was hurt), patrolling an area, and making and receiving calls on a walkie-talkie.

Finding ways to redirect the play is more complicated than just moving the children to another area. Sometimes you may need to shut the play down because it is too disruptive. But if you can build on the interests of the children and redirect the play to a more productive theme, children will use their creativity and imagination in constructive ways.

Time to Reflect

How do you keep children from pretending with guns while they are playing?

_____

_____

_____

_____

Your Reaction to Violent Play

Adults can have a variety of reactions to violent play. Sometimes they are just annoyed that it keeps popping up and feel helpless to stop it. Other times, they may become concerned for the children's safety if they are getting hurt acting out violent themes. If children's play emerges out of trauma, teachers can become worried and distressed.

Talking to Families about Exposure to Violence

Occasionally, you may feel a child is exposed to too much violence on television, in movies, or in video games. This child may talk about it constantly, may be fighting with other children, or may show anxiety about it. You might decide to speak with the family about limiting exposure to violent media. Although it is difficult for families to hear critical feedback about how things are done in their homes, your feedback can help them monitor what their child sees on the screen. Here are some ideas about talking to families about exposure to violence:

- Schedule a time to sit down with the family to talk. Don't use drop-off or pickup times, when the parents are in a hurry.

- Describe how the child is showing distress.

- Share observations or brochures about how violence affects young children.

- Offer suggestions about alternative media for the child.

- Be supportive and offer help.

- Share positive observations of the child as well as the distressed actions of the child.

- Assume all of you are there to help the child and share that assumption with the family.

- Plan a family meeting about how to limit screen time for young children. Families may welcome talking about the topic with other families.

- Be prepared for families to disagree with you. Anticipate how you will respond.

Time to Reflect

What are your concerns when you think of speaking with a family about their child's media exposure?

_____

_____

_____

_____

Which of the suggestions above would you use as you prepare?

_____

_____

_____

_____

Superhero Play

One special type of play that can turn violent is superhero play. Many children watch cartoons and movies with a hero using superpowers to save people from villains. There are the classic superheroes, such as Superman and Batman, but we also have Power Rangers, Teenage Mutant Ninja Turtles, Iron Man, Wolverine, and Spider-Man. Some children have seen zombie movies or television programs and gleefully imitate how zombies walk. When children play superheroes, the play often spirals out of control, especially if it occurs indoors.

Children who are playing their favorite superhero mimic actions they see. So children run, jump from furniture, crawl on furniture, and use exotic weapons. They are able to describe in great detail how the superhero saves people from evil. They incorporate the roles, language, and plot of the story.

Time to Reflect

How do you feel about superhero play in your learning environment? Do you limit it in some way?

_____

_____

_____

_____

Functions of Superhero Play

Although superhero play can lead to violent play, it also serves a function for children. Remember when we discussed why children may be attracted to violent play? These reasons are true for superhero play as well. Children who play superheroes are attracted to this play because they want to feel powerful. Perhaps they are shy or their lives are feeling out of control. Maybe their families are going through stressful times. Engaging in superhero play gives them the feeling that they are all-powerful and can save everyone, including themselves. Superhero play also incorporates the theme of helping others and overcoming adversity to do good. Superhero play can be very beneficial for children if we can find ways to channel the energy. Rather than asking how to stop superhero play, ask yourself how you can shape it to be safe, yet fun and exciting.

Time to Reflect

List the superheroes your children play. What actions do you see that help you understand the characters?

_____

_____

_____

_____

I remember playing G.I. Joe and Davy Crockett. I explored hills, woods, lakeshore, and creek banks with some thought of explorers, pioneers, and Native Americans. I pretended to be an athletic hero with reimaginings of past and present stars of college football, pro baseball, and the Olympics. —Jim S.

Making Rules for Superhero Play

Sit down with your colleagues or fellow providers and list rules that will help children stay safe if they engage in superhero play. Limit the number of rules to two or three. This will make it easier for children to remember. Write them down with the children in large group and discuss each one. Ask yourself these questions: Is there one area you would put aside for superhero play? Would you only want superhero play outside? How should children treat others during superhero play? What kinds of limits would you like to put on superhero play?

Time to Reflect

List rules you would like the children to follow when engaging in superhero play.

_____

_____

_____

_____

Another idea is to ask children to work with you to create the superhero play rules. In a large group, discuss how to keep safe and how to keep others safe. Whether you create the rules with the children or with your team, ask children to make a mark, sign their name, or put their fingerprints on the paper as a way to indicate agreement with the rules.

Remind Children of the Rules When Necessary

Children may get carried away with the story line and forget the rules. Sometimes a reminder can help them pull the excitement back and move the story in a less violent direction.

Join the Superhero Play

By playing a role, you can help shape the direction. Maybe you play a doctor or a firefighter and make suggestions from the perspective of that role. Maybe the children can suggest a role for you. Sometimes they like to "save" their teacher.

Moving Beyond Superhero Play

Superhero play builds on themes of helping others and overcoming challenges. Children sometimes only mimic what they have seen. If they can go beyond the given story and imagine other possibilities, this type of play can be enriching. Draw pictures of the story after playing. Emphasize how the children helped someone and kept trying until they overcame the problem. Provide costumes to strengthen the role play. Introduce new characters into the play to help children go beyond the story line.

Time to Reflect

You listed some of the superheroes your children play. What is the story line they are playing?

_____

_____

_____

_____

What could you add to help children go beyond that story? Think about props, roles, and story line.

_____

_____

_____

_____

Roughhousing during Play

As children grow comfortable with each other, they may express their excitement by pushing, wrestling, and giggling. Although this play isn't rooted in anger or violence, it can become hurtful for the children involved and those around them. Children can be pushed into furniture and hurt themselves. They may misinterpret the actions of the other child and say the child hurt them on purpose. What started out as fun can quickly become a fight. However, this kind of roughhousing can also be a way for children to build friendships if it is channeled into more appropriate play.

☀ Laura was a little nervous. She had just decided to put a new dramatic play theme in her area. She knew some of the children had just been to a parade the week before so thought they would enjoy a parade theme. She made the area bigger to accommodate more children. She brought in boxes to build floats, art materials to decorate the floats, musical instruments for a band, batons, and chairs to set along the parade route. She kept some props back such as banners, hats, and other costumes to introduce at a later time. She introduced the parade at her morning group by asking who had seen the parade. Several children talked about the clowns and the bands. They were especially impressed with the candy thrown from the floats. When she opened the area several children rushed over to play. However, rather than starting to build the floats and decorate them, three of the boys started to push each other. They were laughing and soon were tumbling around the floor. Laura told them they had to leave the area if they were going to act like that. They left the area, laughing and running into one another. Although Laura stayed to help the other children look at the boxes and talk about the floats, she didn't know what to do about the roughhousing. She knew the boys were having fun with each other, but she wanted them to focus enough so they could join the parade.

Time to Reflect

What is your reaction when children are roughhousing in your learning environment? How do you respond to the behavior?

_____

_____

_____

_____

Why Roughhousing Is a Problem

Roughhousing can be difficult to manage because it can be very disruptive. Although our focus is on roughhousing during dramatic play, children rough-house during many times of the day: large group, small group, and other times when you are asking them to pay attention. It may happen over and over again with the same group of children. Although girls do roughhouse and act silly, it is often a behavior associated with groups of boys. Sometimes when the roughhousing escalates, children can get hurt and conflicts can arise.

Reasons Children Roughhouse

Sometimes we don't look closely at why children roughhouse because we are stressed and irritated. Roughhousing serves several purposes for children. Here are some of them:

- They may be excited by a new friendship.
- They may be forming friendships as a group.
- They may not know what role to play with the new theme.
- They may be overexcited because of a holiday, birthday, or special event.
- They may be active children who need to move frequently.
- They may be mimicking interactions they have seen.
- The theme itself may be an exciting one.

What You Might See When Children Are Roughhousing

Usually roughhousing is easy to spot. You might see some of the following behaviors:

- children pushing and shoving each other
- children laughing as they tussle
- children ignoring your requests to stop or attempts to redirect them
- children wrestling on the ground

Time to Reflect

Think of a time you have seen children dissolving into this kind of silly, roughhousing type of play. Why do you think they might do this?

_____

_____

_____

_____

Redirecting Roughhousing

To address roughhousing in the dramatic play area, think of ways to redirect the play. Roughhousing can be positive for children. It helps them bond with each other and form friendships. It gets out some of the energy young children carry. Boys, in particular, bond with friends in this manner. By redirecting this behavior into positive avenues, children can still use energy, form friendships, and have fun within a supportive structure. Here are some ideas:

- Look at the amount of space you have for your dramatic play. Too much space can encourage roughhousing and running.
- Use outside play to extend the theme. For example, perhaps Laura can take the parade outside some days.
- Give each child a role to play, particularly in the beginning.
- Offer exciting dramatic play themes where children work together to battle a common threat such as preparing for a storm or crossing over hot lava.
- Tolerate a little roughhousing if it ends quickly. Sometimes when teachers ignore it, it ends.
- Give children a space to roughhouse away from the other children. Set rules to keep all safe.

- Let children engage in more running, silliness, and roughhousing outside. Supervise carefully to ensure children are following the rules you have set.
- Be supportive when you have to stop the roughhousing because it is getting out of hand. Let children know you want them to have fun and will find something else they can do together.

Your Reaction to Roughhousing

You plan based on goals you want to accomplish. However, your goals may not always match the children's goals. Although the boys were attracted to the parade theme, they clearly were more interested in the roughhousing. Teachers often say they can see where this type of play is going. In other words, they see it escalating and someone getting hurt. They find it hard to stop once it starts.

Children's violent play is often a focus of teachers' complaints. When children reenact violent themes or imitate superheroes they can hurt others. Even roughhousing can disrupt peaceful play. If you redirect the play into related themes instead of stopping it altogether, you will be more successful. Children often play violently because of what they see, but also because of how it makes them feel. When they are acting out a superhero role, they feel powerful and in control. When they are roughhousing, they are connecting with other children. Give them alternative ways to feel confident, successful, and connected.

Time to Reflect

Complete the following sentences:

When children are roughhousing, I feel like

_____

_____

I usually

_____

_____

Instead, I will

_____

_____

Redirecting this type of play can be very difficult. What play theme could you try that could channel this behavior? Keep in mind that it would need to be active and involve more than one child.

_____

_____

_____

_____

Opening Up Play Opportunities CHAPTER 8

No matter what your role is with children, you will encounter children who love playing and eagerly seek out other children to join. You will also see children having a hard time playing together. They may not engage in the dramatic play area, they may have conflicts, they may play violently, or they may play the same thing over and over again. These are typical challenges you encounter when you work with young children. Even though they are typical, these challenges may keep children from gaining the most they can from their play experiences. Your thoughtful response to these challenges can open up opportunities for children, rather than close them. Through your use of exciting dramatic play themes matched to your units or themes, you open up children's imaginative thinking and provide opportunities for them to learn to play. When you introduce new props and unfamiliar play themes, they learn new information. When you introduce the problem-solving techniques to the children and provide space and time for them to practice, they become more able to apply these skills when you aren't there. Aiming for an environment free of conflict or challenges is not the goal. The goal is to teach ways to solve the conflicts and challenges so that children learn to solve their own conflicts in peaceful ways.

When you are experiencing children's play challenges, think about the following:

Reflect on your environment. Observe how children are using your environment. Make sure the children have enough props that are interesting and engaging. Vary your dramatic play themes. Provide interest areas that are defined and appropriately sized for the types of play you expect in that area. Include props that are realistic as well as more abstract ones. Be sure to include math and literacy props in each play theme. Find ways to move dramatic play outside.

Reflect on the children in your group. Make sure you are providing opportunities for several stages of play: solitary, parallel, and cooperative. Think about children's experiences in their homes and neighborhoods. Do your props reflect their cultural experiences? If they aren't responding to the play environment, try to decide whether the children are bored, restless, or developmentally not ready to participate in your play themes.

Reflect on your reactions. Reflect on your reactions to the play challenges as well as your feelings while dealing with the issues. Your reactions can feed negativity or anxiety. You may find that the tensions between the children are lessened when you examine your feelings and responses and work to change them.

Identify the challenge and apply problem-solving steps. Spend some time identifying the challenge. By defining it clearly you will spend less time on the problem-solving steps. Think about your experiences with this challenge in the past. What you learned may help you come up with ideas. Reflect on the interests and strengths of the children in your group and include this assessment in the plan.

Evaluate how your strategy is working. Observe the children during play and decide if your idea is working or if you need to change course. Talk with your teammates or other providers to get their ideas and observations.

Acknowledge success. When you see improvement in the children's abilities to solve conflicts or engage in play, let them know you notice that improvement. Give yourself a much deserved pat on the back. Remember that successful strategy for future use.

Practice Problem-Solving Play Challenges

We have described several kinds of group play challenges you may see in your learning environment. Think of a problem you have been having with groups of children. Then go through the problem-solving steps outlined in the first part of the book.

Time to Reflect

Identify the problem. What is the problem?

_____

_____

_____

_____

Gather information. What did you observe? What was your reaction?

_____

_____

_____

_____

Brainstorm solutions.

_____

_____

_____

_____

Pick the best idea. What will you try?

_____

_____

_____

_____

Try it. Try the idea for at least two weeks. Is the problem improving? How are the children responding?

_____

_____

_____

_____

Decide if it is working. Is the problem getting better?

_____

_____

_____

_____

Revise if needed. Do you need to revise or change some part of the idea? What would it be?

_____

_____

_____

_____

Reflecting on the Children in Your Group

Children engage in play more when they are interested in the theme, the props, and the roles. When you think of the children in your group, how would you fill in the following spaces? What are their favorite props? What are their favorite play themes? What are their favorite roles?

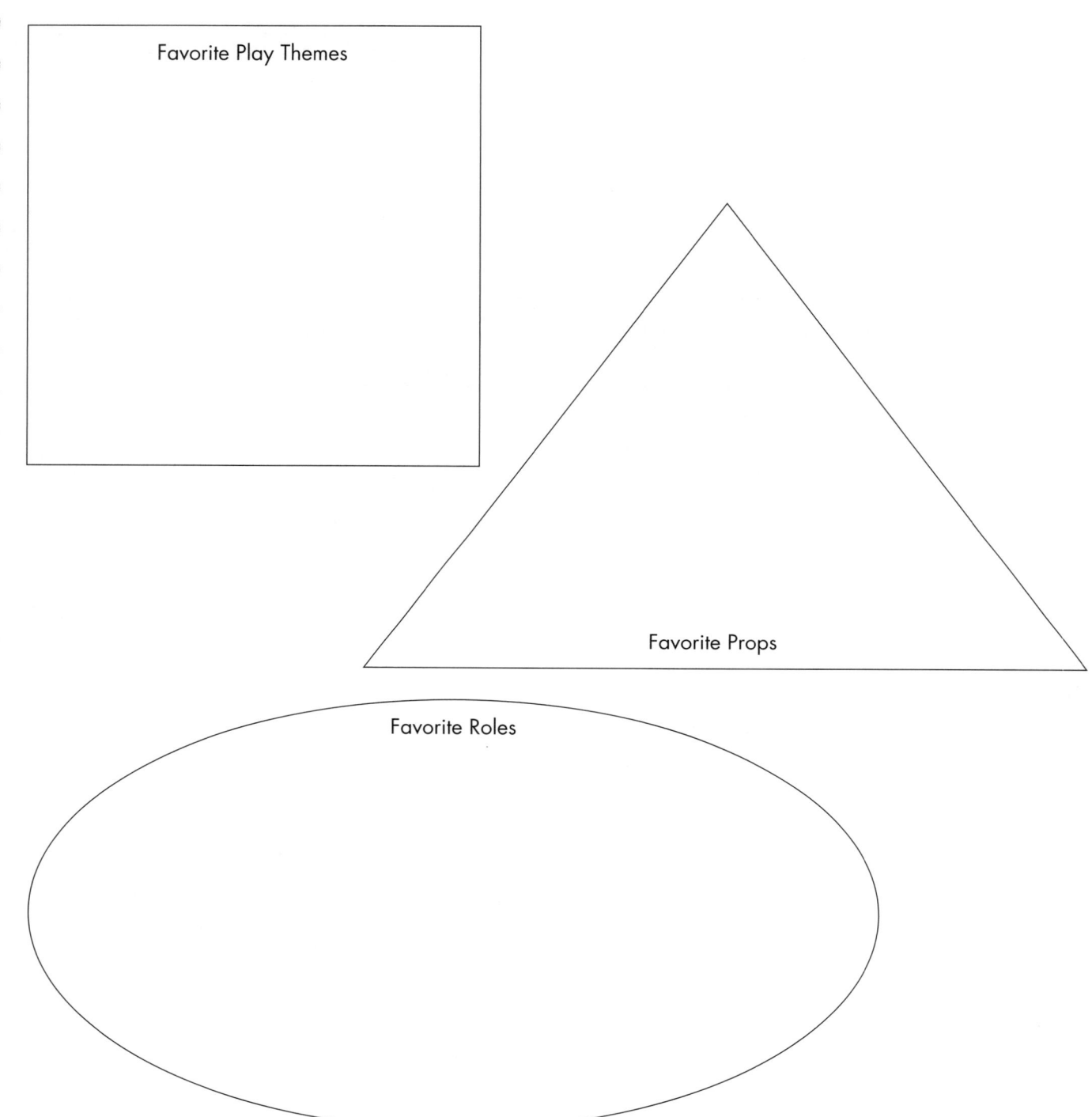

Favorite Play Themes

Favorite Props

Favorite Roles

I remember a parachute being donated to my children's preschool. I wanted so to join in on that play experience. I wondered, "What will they learn?". . . I will always look for projects/programs that encourage teaching creativity and outside the box thinking. I want to see a parachute in a classroom again. —Sameerah

Even though part of this book's focus has been on the challenges you see in children's play, remember how fun play can be for them. It is easy to lose sight of that as you deal with the day-to-day conflicts and problems that come up between children. By remembering your own childhood play experiences, you have more empathy for the children's play experiences. When you match your props and themes to the children's development levels, you give them security and confidence. When you facilitate exciting dramatic play themes, you give children new experiences to ponder. When you observe children in conflict and help them find a solution, you teach them new skills to try when they are upset. By helping them engage in play and broaden their play themes beyond imitative superhero play, you bring new energy to their play.

The next book, *When Play Isn't Easy: Helping Children Enter and Sustain Play*, covers play and learning standards and how you define and communicate the value of play. It explores the challenges individual children may have with learning play skills and looks at strategies you can use to help the child learn that, when all is said and done, play is fun.

I still see lots of creative and imaginative play. I think children are always practicing the skills they see adults using and trying on different roles they can play. My youngest grandson, who is ten years old, still loves stuffed animals and sleeps with herds of them—it isn't all electronics. —JoAnn

Time to Reflect

Go back to the beginning of the book and read through the self-assessment you completed in the introduction. Describe two important things you have learned from this book.

_____

_____

_____

_____